Sunny St.

THE THERADELIC APPROACH

THE THERADELIC APPROACH

Psychedelic Therapy

Perspective, Preparation, and Practice

Sunny Strasburg, LMFT

Foreword by Dr. Richard Schwartz, Ph.D.

ABOUT THE AUTHOR

SUNNY STRASBURG, LMFT, is a licensed and certified psychedelic trainer, consultant, therapist, author, presenter, psychotherapist, and entrepreneur. She is an EMDR-certified trauma specialist, experienced and certified in psychedelic-assisted psychotherapy, and trained in Internal Family Systems (IFS). A Certification for Psychedelic-Assisted Therapy graduate from the California Institute of Integral Studies, Sunny is trained in ketamine, MDMA by MAPS, and psilocybin-assisted psychotherapies by Synthesis and Compass Pathways.

Sunny is the Clinical Director at TRIPP PsyAssist, developing virtual reality and mobile app support for psychedelic therapists. Sunny was a senior trainer at the Ketamine Training Center and has cofacilitated KAP training and retreats with Richard Schwartz, Bessel Van der Kolk, and other leaders in psychedelic and trauma psychology.

Sunny specializes in attachment trauma, using an eclectic approach with the Gottman Couples Method, Jungian, and Depth Psychology. She offers ketamine-assisted therapy with individual sessions and group therapy retreats. Sunny has developed original protocols using ketamine-assisted therapy and other trauma treatment methods, which she presents at conferences such as SXSW, the Expanded States of Consciousness World Summit, Psychedelics Today podcast, the EMDRIA Worldwide Virtual Conference, EMDR UK, and the Boston Trauma Conference.

TABLE OF CONTENTS

SECTION THREE

FOREWORD

I'm excited about this book for several reasons. First, I've co-led with the author several retreats that combined ketamine with the psychotherapy I developed called Internal Family Systems (IFS). In each, I found Sunny to be one of the most compassionate, creative, and connected (what, in IFS, we call Self-led) leaders I've worked with. In addition, she knows more about all kinds of psychedelics and how to use them safely and therapeutically than anyone I've met. Finally, I am honored that she has embraced IFS as both her primary map to the psychedelic territory and the primary method for healing the emotions and sensations that emerge during psychedelic experiences. (She artfully incorporates aspects of EMDR and archetypal psychology, but IFS is the primary framework).

Our retreats have been extraordinary. When I first agreed to experiment with combining IFS and ketamine, I had low expectations. I thought, "In general, we do fine with straight IFS, but sometimes we get stuck, and maybe this will help with that." After the first couple of days, however, I was blown away! The ketamine seemed to put the parts of participants that manage their lives ordinarily (manager protectors) to sleep, which releases a huge amount of what we call Self energy—they suddenly felt large amounts of the eight C words of Self: calm, confidence, curious, compassionate, courage, creativity, clarity and connectedness. That open, loving state then invited parts of them their managers had locked away to be seen and helped. In some cases, in fifteen minutes, we could heal what might take five ordinary IFS sessions to even get to. Some participants also began to have what seemed to be spiritual experiences. They would meet entities that gave them wisdom about and perspective on their lives that they experienced as coming into them rather than from within them.

Also, the retreat groups became extremely close and connected in a short period, as if each participant was touching into the larger Self of the group and, consequently, extending full support for the healing of one another. This carpet of loving Self energy and connectedness becomes a foundation of safety and trust that allows for deep access and quick transformation of burdened parts.

We also found in the pre-medicine prep sessions, that, by encouraging participants to listen inside and find protectors that were afraid to do the medicine and then address those fears until the protectors felt reassured, participants had smoother but also more fertile medicine sessions.

After several of these retreats it's become clear to me that ketamine can have the effect of enhancing and expediting IFS sessions and making them more spiritual. Hence my excitement about this book because, in it, Sunny covers all of these practices and more. She also provides an eloquent, philosophical, and historical introduction to the use of ketamine and of psychedelics in general.

Sunny makes profound statements, such as:

"We need a new guiding ethic that makes sense for these times—one that transcends humans as the most important species and views the entire earth and all sentient beings as possessing consciousness and being worthy of empathy. Psychedelics can be a part of this new vision. They offer the direct sense that we belong to a collective tribe and are part of nature..."

And:

"Once in a while, I will have a psychedelic journey so incredibly profound that I can't help but believe other realities exist; they exist and function whether or not I am there to witness them. Sentient beings are going on with their lives, suddenly noticing and taking a sincere interest in me. Psychedelic visions contain creatures beckoning and celebrating my arrival. There is no way my brain could fabricate this. I must be discovering another plane of reality that exists independently..."

My years of experience doing IFS have led me to the same conclusion—that there are independent other worlds that parts and other beings exist in and that we can enter when we focus inside, even without psychedelics. She invites us to become more ensouled and makes it clear that the mystical side of psychedelic experiences should not be downplayed even as scientists offer mundane explanations and practices and businesses look to profit.

In addition, however, Sunny gets pragmatic, with lots of advice, coming from her decades of experience, about how to create the best set and setting and what kind of pitfalls to avoid. From instructions on creating treatment protocols to what kind of music is best, she covers the territory thoroughly.

In the third section, she goes into some detail regarding how to combine IFS and ketamine. The word *psychedelic* translates to "mind manifesting." If, as I do, you consider the mind to be populated with parts, then the medicine is manifesting your parts, which is what so many leaders in the field of psychedelics report—that parts pop up spontaneously all the time.

As I discussed above, Self is also manifested spontaneously. If you are interested in exploring the territory that emerges when mind is manifest this way, then it helps to have a non-pathologizing, clear map to the territory that leads to profound healing. IFS is such a map, and I'm grateful to Sunny for holding it up for you in such a clear and empowering way. She also gracefully combines IFS with her previous frameworks of Jungian archetypal psychology and EMDR.

Richard Schwartz, Ph.D.

ACKNOWLEDGMENTS

I couldn't have written this book without the incredible wisdom and support of my husband and co-adventurer in life, Martin Stensaas. Thank you for your support, patience, and tremendous knowledge of psychedelics, neurophysiology, and philosophy. Special thanks go to Dr. Richard Schwartz for his guidance and expertise. I will be forever grateful to you, Dick. Thank you to Dr. Jeffrey Becker, M.D., for contributing to psychedelic medicines' history and neurophysiologic effects, and to my editors, Deborah Emmit and Jane Gerhard.

HOW TO USE THIS BOOK

This book is for mental healthcare clinicians. It is also helpful for those interested in finding a well-trained psychedelic-assisted psychotherapist. It is a guide to offering a proper set, setting, and complementary therapeutic methods for adequately integrating the psychedelic experience. However, a straightforward workbook on how to set up a psychedelic therapy practice couldn't capture the essence of doing great work with psychedelic medicine. The chemist who discovered LSD, Albert Hofmann, said psychedelic medicines are a "nonspecific amplifier of the unconscious" (Hofmann 2009). Because psychedelics tend to be nonlinear, qualitative, and wonderfully archetypal, I feel compelled to pull the lens back for a more inclusive philosophical and psychosocial view.

Additionally, mental health is deeply affected by assumptions and narratives ingrained in contemporary culture. Psychedelics offer us one of the most hopeful potentials: a sense of value, meaning, and purpose. They are not a panacea for our current ills but provide a doorway to a relevant, collective spirituality and sense of value. They can serve as a theoretical framework that holds up to the scrutiny of the modern age by still having the ability to fill us with wonder and a sense of connection. Could the psychedelic renaissance inspire a new, global mythology? Could we transcend commodified, post-humanism and science fueled by capitalism and move toward a new, life-affirming integration that infuses everything with meaning and sentience?

I have organized this book into three main sections. The first section is a larger view of our culture, exploring philosophy, art, and psychedelics. The second section looks at specific psychedelics and some of the mentors and teachers who have influenced me to create the Theradelic Approach. The third section looks at the Theradelic Approach in more detail and offers guidance on conducting psychedelic therapy sessions. Please read the entire book for an in-depth journey, or jump to the sections that interest you most.

Several mentors I have had the opportunity to work with have profoundly inspired me. They have included Dr. Richard Schwartz, the Internal Family Systems (IFS) originator, Drs. John and Julie Gottman, founders of the Gottman Method, Dr. Bessel van der Kolk, trauma specialist, and Dr. William Richards, one of the early researchers of psilocybin, and many others.

I have woven many of the most relevant tools for psychedelic therapy into the Theradelic Approach, including IFS, EMDR, attachment theory, and depth psychology. I intend this book to supplement training in these specific methodologies and hope it will inspire you to seek in-depth training. Please see the Resources section for websites that provide more information.

SECTION ONE

1
INTRODUCTION TO THE THERADELIC APPROACH

thera: treating disease and promoting healing
delic: manifesting
Theradelic Approach: promoting the manifestation of healing

In recent years, as the psychedelic field has blossomed, there has been an increasingly urgent need for well-trained therapists who are skilled, experienced, and, most importantly, who uphold best-practice standards. Creating a qualitative model and turning it into quantitative training is challenging. Psychology is a science and an art. How can we train people to maintain integrity? How do we convey the importance of therapists receiving therapy to prevent a lack of self-awareness from negatively impacting clients?

In this book, I offer a broader context and specific guidance to inspire you to absorb this material, directly experience psychedelics yourself, and do your own processing in personal psychotherapy. Hopefully, this will translate the qualitative experience of being a great therapist into a practical guide.

This book offers guidance about becoming a knowledgeable psychedelic therapist, conducting therapy sessions, and using complementary therapeutic modalities such as Internal Family Systems (IFS), archetypal psychology, and EMDR to increase the effectiveness and safety of psychedelic therapy sessions.

2

NEW NARRATIVE MYTHOLOGY: CONNECTING US MORE DEEPLY TO OUR NATURE, ONE ANOTHER, AND THE NATURAL WORLD

"The potential for the beneficial use of psychedelics is enormous, but we need to be careful to use them in a responsible and intentional way. They are powerful tools that can lead to profound insights and healing, but they must be approached with respect and caution, and used in a safe and supportive environment. When used in this way, psychedelics can be transformative and life-changing."

—RICK DOBLIN,
FOUNDER AND EXECUTIVE DIRECTOR
OF THE MULTIDISCIPLINARY ASSOCIATION
FOR PSYCHEDELIC STUDIES (MAPS)

The Theradelic Approach is a practical guide to working with psychedelic medicines. It is an introduction for therapists interested in becoming psychedelic therapists and knowing how to become properly trained and experienced in offering these incredible tools. I will describe techniques to get you started, but no book can replace in-person, experiential training in psychedelic-assisted psychotherapy.

This book is also for people interested in psychedelic therapy for their own mental health and wellness. It will help you understand what to look for in a psychedelic therapist.

Alongside the practical nature of this book, it is essential to discuss creating a new narrative mythology that connects us more deeply to our true nature, one another, and the natural world. I would be remiss if I didn't situate this work in a more extensive view that considers philosophical assumptions and mystical insights.

Humans have always deified what we cannot control: nature, our uncontrollable desires, and death. We have always created a personalized, mythological structure for making sense of our mystical experiences. Myth and mysticism are legitimate topics to explore, as humans are hardwired to create stories and seek meaning to make sense of our world. Mystical experiences have occurred through the ages and in all cultures; they are part of our human heritage. As a society, we need to admit mystical experiences are valuable and worthwhile for the collective. We are now finding through empirical research that mystical experiences have concrete positive outcomes in clinical settings. This structure can guide us toward healing our psyches and perhaps that of all other sentient beings with whom we share the world.

Loss of Soul: A Personal and Cultural Dislocation

Many of us in the modern world feel disconnected from purpose and meaning. This alienation is reflected personally on an individual scale and culturally in the more extensive social system. As a remedy, psychedelic therapy can reimbue us with a sense of purpose and reconnect us with the numinous. James Hillman, an American psychologist, author, and lecturer known for his work in archetypal psychology, says a person's distress indicates an imaginal imbalance of psychospiritual "dislocation from the source" (Hillman 1996). This dislocation suggests a person has lost their connection to their inner and outer mythopoetic realms, and they feel as if they have "lost their souls."

Hillman's work focuses on the power of imagination and the role of the psyche in personal growth and healing. He states, "By soul, I mean, first of all, a perspective rather than a substance, a viewpoint toward things rather than a thing itself. This perspective is reflective; it mediates events and makes differences between ourselves and everything that happens. There is a reflective moment between us and events, between the doer and the deed, and soul-making means differentiating this middle ground" (Hillman 1989, 20).

He goes on to talk about the individual. "Without his soul, he has lost a sense of belonging and the sense of being in communion with the powers of the gods. His personal myths and his connection to the larger myth of his people as *raison d'être* is lost" (18). This imbalance is not only individually psychopathological but indicative of broader societal detachment patterns from formerly unconscious and uniform cultural mythos and ethos. As C.G. Jung says about the modern condition:

> For the collective psyche shows the same pattern of change as the psyche of the individual. So long as all goes well and all our psychic energies find an outlet in adequate and well-regulated ways, we are disturbed by nothing from within. No uncertainty or doubt besets us, and we cannot be divided against ourselves. But no sooner are one or two channels of psychic activity blocked up than phenomena of obstruction appear. The stream tries to flow back against the current, the inner man wants something different than the outer man, and we are at war with ourselves. Only then, in the situation of distress, do we discover the psyche as something that thwarts our will, which is strange and even hostile to us, and which is incompatible with our conscious standpoint (Jung 1957, 463–464).

Not surprisingly, this general predicament often describes the psychological starting point and ambiance of distress clinicians frequently see in the psychotherapeutic setting.

Cultural Polarizations and Hubris

Like most people in the modern world, I experience bouts of intense existential angst. Part of me is white-knuckling through life, waiting for it to "get back to normal." But the problem is, we no longer know what normal is. Modern humans simultaneously depend upon and feel alienated by the world in which we live. This new world is polarized, high-tech, high-stress, socially isolated, polluted, and heavily mediated. We can't escape because we are captured and carried along like an amusement park ride with too much plastic, media, and propaganda.

Political polarization is at an apex. Politically, philosophically, and spiritually, the two sides are pulling into further and further opposition. In one camp is the desire to return to a simpler time (that never actually existed). This retrogressive religious and conservative world feels safe and familiar (for the small, chosen in-group). This position tries to push the perceived outsiders to the other side of the proverbial white picket fence. What appears as an opposing camp desires to hurl us headlong into technology, science, and materialism, hoping these changes will resolve stubborn problems. They say, "Let's build a rocket to go live on Mars!" (again, only if you are part of the small, chosen in-group). Instead of an old-world god coming to rescue us from ourselves, the new faith offers silicon-based artificial intelligence and science as our new-world gods. These polarized stances are two sides of the same coin—to escape what is happening now.

We have a new question that we have never had to ask before: "What is reality?" Life is getting more complicated, blurring reality with artificial intelligence, technology, and psychedelics. Time is speeding up, and our natural world looks more alien and less predictable in the face of climate crises. A proliferation of reality narratives is popping up to meet the challenges of making sense of the world. These conceptualized realities range from flat-earthers accelerating the apocalypse to Silicon Valley technologists asserting that humans live in a solipsistic simulation game that alien teenagers created billions of years in the future. They posit that humans are merely SIMs.

We no longer have nature as a constant context for relating to ourselves and the world around us. The rhythms and limitations of prior ages have been lost. Instead, we navigate our days detached from nature, from our tribe. Held within our cubicle houses, we rattle from one room, where we work on a computer screen all day, to another room at night, if we're lucky enough to have two rooms where we eat and sleep. The climate we reside in most of the time isn't natural. It is air-conditioned and heated to keep us oblivious to what is happening outside. Rather than looking out over the vista at the sun dipping below the horizon, we stare at a glowing computer screen with a color-enhanced photo of a sunset. Adding to the confusion, media makers recognize the lack of collective meaning. They can't resist seizing the opportunity to capitalize on the fear and discontent. They desire power over a culture desperate for a unified mythology. Propaganda and misinformation add layers of doubt and dissociation to our consciousness.

Over time, duty and responsibility have forced cultures to develop wisdom and restraint. But these qualities limit industries that thrive on alienation, impulsivity, and indulgence—all qualities of an immature psyche. Modern culture and artificial intelligence have been developed mainly by a culture that Jung termed the *puer*. In mythology, the puer is a child god who is forever young. For Jungians, the term describes an older person whose emotional life has remained at an adolescent's developmental level. Perpetual adolescence is also known as "Peter Pan syndrome." The puer tends to lead a "provisional life," scared of being caught in a situation from which it might not be possible to escape. They seek independence and freedom, oppose boundaries and limits, and tend to find any restriction intolerable. Many modern people are trapped in a puer complex. We only need to look at social media for confirmation of this. Is it any wonder men of the high-tech age emulate insecure boys building phallus-shaped rockets to Mars?

"They want to recreate the womb!" As Timothy Leary, the psychologist, saw it, the boys building our digital future were developing technology to simulate the ideal woman, the one their mothers could never be. Unlike the human mother who failed them, a predictive algorithm could anticipate their every need in advance, and deliver it directly, removing every trace of friction and longing. These guys would be able to float fully fed and serviced in their virtual bubbles, what the media lab called "artificial ecology" (Rushkoff 2022).

People, animals, plants, and even entire ecosystems have perished under regimes of organized religion, warring autocracies, propaganda, and disinformation. In much of the West, we now live in a post-Christian, post-humanist era without a guiding ethic to unify humanity. According to the most recent U.S. census, atheism has increased by twelve percent in the last decade. The shared bonds of old-world religions are dissolving, climate apocalypse is upon us, and AI threatens to amplify the worst of our modern culture. Is it any wonder depression, anxiety, and trauma are worldwide epidemics? Jiddu Krishnamurti says, "It is no measure of health to be well adjusted to a profoundly sick society." It is time we examined a larger view and asked ourselves why we are perpetuating a reality that leaves us feeling alienated and fractured from ourselves, one another, nature, mysticism, and the earth itself.

The one thing we might turn to as a constant reality—that we can all agree upon because it is replicable—is science. During the last few centuries, science became the gold standard that provided a consensual reality to return to collectively. But even science is being questioned by the masses. Populists now promote propaganda to discredit science to keep the carbon/capitalist machine grinding along to maintain the status quo. Unfortunately, like its technological fruits, the research industry has also been co-opted by capitalism. As the stresses of capitalism advance, mistrust deepens within popular culture. The "haves" exploit the "have-nots" with new science-based technological efficiencies. Rather than having a nuanced conversation about the data and its best use, each group holes up in its polarized camp, insisting the other side is insane. Payouts, grants, and investors seeking specific research outcomes skew the intent of science and technology. In the scientific method, one must always question the presuppositions and what we are asking, as well as review the data soberly and without cognitive bias. How many people are educated enough to do this?

Each of us has an outcome we desire. We will never get a big enough lens, with enough perspective, to truly understand "reality." We have access to more information than we have ever had, and yet somehow, culture is collectively devolving to be more insular, insipid, narcissistic, and ignorant. Some hope it will be the artificial intelligence beings who will set us straight. However, the reality is that such a hope opens us to new dangers based on unexamined desires and entrenched expectations. The problem with losing our collective mythology—humanism—is that it's not being replaced with any new paradigm to give us collective meaning and direction. The apocalyptic fever dream devolves into delusions of apathy and despair.

We need a new guiding ethic that makes sense for these times—one that transcends humans as the most important species and views the entire earth and all sentient beings as possessing consciousness and being worthy of empathy. Psychedelics can be a part of this new vision. They offer the direct sense that we belong to a collective tribe and are part of nature. Humans need a collective mythology to survive. We need other community members to check on us, to keep us engaged and accountable to one another and the greater world.

One of our most fundamental human talents is telling stories to seek and apply meaning to a chaotic world. It's our poetic way of navigating reality and making sense of events. Storymaking is essential to provide meaning and hope, but we also tend to use stories to perpetuate denial and engage in magical thinking. Scores of cognitive biases show that our talent for narrative is fraught with pitfalls. Religion and tech culture contain hidden fairy tales of waiting for a supernatural angel to save us from self-destruction. It's a powerful projection of wishing our parents would come into our room, turn on the nightlight, and rescue us from our nightmares. Maybe no one is coming to save us, and it is time to transcend the puer complex and become adults who take accountability for our actions, policies, technologies, and consequences.

There are times when I am rattled out of this denatured modern fever dream, however. After an epic ayahuasca journey in the jungle, or the time I had a near-death experience, or standing breathless at an epic view of the mountains after a long day's hike, I am certain consciousness exists outside my skull, and magic abounds. Love and meaning infuse in everything; my life is a prayer of compassion. I become a goddess, pure, with unlimited consciousness of equal importance to every leaf, rock, and animal. The separation of inside and outside is gone; all is a continuum of beauty and grace. These precious moments of pure awareness have become the compass for my life. In the chaos of this world, deep within myself, there is an ability to contact the numinous, eternal truth. Sometimes these peak experiences happen to us, and often we seek them out. We open ourselves and our psyches to grace and profound presence. "Psyche" is not simply "mind." Psyche is ensouled awareness.

In 1957 Humphrey Osmond coined the term "psychedelic" in "A Review of the Clinical Effects of Psychotomimetic Agents." His musings on the importance of psychedelics are just as relevant today. This passage is from *Annals of the New York Academy of Sciences*:

> I have tried to find an appropriate name for the agents under discussion: a name that will include the concepts of enriching the mind and enlarging the vision. Some possibilities are psychephoric, mind-moving; psychehormic, mind-rousing; and psycheplastic, mind-molding. Psychezymic, mind-fermenting, is indeed appropriate. Psycherhexic, mind bursting forth, though difficult, is memorable. Psychelytic, mind-releasing, is satisfactory. My choice,

because it is clear, euphonious, and uncontaminated by other associations, is psychedelic, mind-manifesting. One of these terms should serve.

This, then, is how one clinician sees these psychedelics. I believe these agents play a part in our survival as a species. For that survival depends as much on our opinion of our fellows and ourselves as on any other single thing. The psychedelics help us to explore and fathom our own nature (Osmond 1957).

Psychedelics help us explore and fathom our own nature, which relieves burnt-out healthcare workers who want to feel more effective at alleviating their patients' distress. I have been a psychotherapist for nearly two decades. I'm a psychedelic therapist specializing in trauma and a trainer who teaches psychedelic therapy to licensed health and mental healthcare workers. I have noticed the paradox of healers trying to help others while they remain unhealed themselves. The burnout seems to appear everywhere, in my therapy clients' struggles, friends' laments, colleagues complaining about working with traumatized and stressed-out populations, politics, and the media. We are all burned out. We need a new way, or maybe an old way renewed and approached with fresh eyes.

Limitations of Reductivist Science

> *Nature is often hidden,*
> *sometimes overcome, seldom extinguished.*
>
> —SIR FRANCIS BACON

In Western thought, there has long been a narrative that nature is to be controlled and subjugated. Western science was incubated within the scholarly traditions of Judeo-Christianity. It has sought to control and explain away what is unpredictable and unknown, whether it be magic, nature, or spirit. With this comes the idea that there is one god and one truth at which we will eventually arrive. The Bible asserts a rational and benevolent god created a natural world that could be studied and understood through reason and observation. This assertion provided the transition to the scientific method.

Furthermore, the biblical idea of a created world distinct from its creator, and the belief that the natural world is a rational and orderly place, shaped how early scientists approached their work. Before René Descartes, science and religion were a continuum. Practices like alchemy were as much mysticism as they were science.

The roots of our alienation and the difficulty of creating meaning and connection are deep and started centuries ago. The earliest examples of merging science with spirituality are found in the work of medieval scholastic philosophers, many of whom were also theologians. These thinkers, such as Thomas Aquinas, developed a rational and systematic approach to understanding the natural world, drawing heavily on the biblical and Aristotelian traditions. They believed that the natural world was a reflection of God's wisdom and that by studying it, they could gain knowledge of God.

We find another example in the work of Sir Francis Bacon in the 1600s, who is considered one of the founders of modern science. He believed a rational god created the natural world and could be studied and understood through reason and observation. Eventually, the scientific method became the new power structure that religious institutions had previously held. Science advanced humanism and technology. Sir Francis Bacon said, "I am come in very truth, leading to your nature with all her children to bind her to your service and make her your slave." We cannot "expect nature to come to us [...] Nature must be taken by the forelock. It is necessary to subdue her, to shake her to her foundations" (1620). This mistrust of nature, the feminine, and anything uncontrollable and unknown continues today in modern science. If we could subdue the unknown by isolating, quantifying, and denaturing everything down to simple, observable phenomena, we would understand everything. We would finally be able to control our destiny. Reductivist materialism doesn't prove that nature is void of sentience and numinosity.

Bacon's violent arrogance toward nature and its mysteries gained increasing acceptance as the scientific revolution was built upon the Age of Enlightenment. As the reliability of scientific inquiry began to increasingly become more convincing than religious dogmas, there was an inevitable divorce of scientific rationalism from traditional approaches to knowledge. As scientific rationalism advanced the standing of the individual and their power to inquire and test knowledge, that also laid the groundwork for the Romantic Movement to create an aura of individual discovery. Nineteenth-century German philosopher Friedrich Nietzsche's philosophy can be seen as a response to his time's intellectual and cultural trends, which included not only Romanticism but also the rise of science, secularism, and skepticism. While he was influenced by Romantic thinkers, he ultimately rejected many of their core ideas and developed a unique philosophical perspective that had a profound impact on Western thought. The statement "God is dead" in his book *Thus Spoke Zarathustra* (1883) expresses Nietzsche's belief that traditional religious beliefs and values had lost their power and relevance in the modern world. Nietzsche believed that the death of God represented the end of conventional morality and the need for people to create new values and beliefs for themselves. The phrase is a critique of Christianity and its moral absolutes. However, materialism makes a thanatophoric death god that reduces everything to dead commodities and abstract fungible value. This nihilism hasn't brought modern humans any collective peace.

Even today, we see this fetish with denaturing everything. For example, some pharmaceutical companies are trying to remove the psychedelic, mystical experience from psychedelics and retain only the anti-depressant effects. I share the sentiment of many psychonauts who find this deeply offensive. Why remove and denature an essential component of the psychedelic experience? Why rob us of the relief of realizing we don't know everything and that it is impossible to control nature? There is great comfort in surrendering to the realization that the universe isn't empty, chaotic, and void of consciousness. We can directly experience the world as numinous. It is alive, wise, and full of wonder. Research has shown that the mystical experience can produce enduring therapeutic results, often described as a sense of oneness with everything. Studies have found that people who have had a mystical experience, whether through psychedelic or nonpharmacological means, report a decrease in symptoms related to mental health conditions such as depression, anxiety, and post-traumatic stress disorder (PTSD) (Griffiths et al. 2006; Ross et al. 2016). Additionally, research indicates that people who have had a mystical experience often report long-term positive changes. They encounter shifts in attitudes, values, and behaviors, such as an increased sense of meaning and purpose and a greater feeling of self-awareness (Johnson et al. 2011; MacLean, Johnson, and Griffiths 2011; Pahnke et al. 1969). These findings suggest that mystical experiences may have a profound and lasting impact on an individual's emotional and psychological well-being.

Yet, modern Westerners do not feel comfortable trusting there is a conscious intelligence much greater than ourselves. This trust goes against the atomistic individualism of our age. But perhaps this is also why, when we have an overwhelming psychedelic experience, we often emerge to find incredible relief and healing. We can't hold on to our conventional sense of a separate identity nor assure ourselves we are ultimately in control. Our intellect, and even our definition of "who we are," dissolve when the psychedelic forces us to surrender to something more splendid, wiser, and more powerful than ourselves. In that surrender, paradoxically, we find incredible relief and freedom. The profound submission to something much more significant than us directing all of life is often incredibly soothing and invigorating.

We are hardwired to need a mythology that directs us, cares for us, provides meaning, and helps us feel safe in our place in the world. In the brilliant book *Sapiens: A Brief History of Humankind*, Yuval Harari describes humans as half-evolved organisms, not strictly predators and not exactly prey either. This partial evolution has created an insecure animal that tends toward violence to overcome insecurity. We mistake the overcompensating desire for power as the most critical factor. Collectively, we are similar to teenagers who think they are indestructible. We are not beyond reproach, nor are we unassailable.

This is a key to understanding our history and psychology. Genus *Homo*'s position in the food chain was, until quite recently, solidly in the middle. For millions of years, humans hunted smaller creatures and gathered what they could, all the while being hunted by larger predators. It was only 400,000 years ago that several species of man began to hunt large game on a regular basis, and only in the last 100,000 years — with the rise of *Homo sapiens* — that man jumped to the top of the food chain. That spectacular leap from the middle to the top had enormous consequences. Other animals at the top of the pyramid, such as lions and sharks, evolved into that position very gradually, over millions of years. This enabled the ecosystem to develop checks and balances that prevent lions and sharks from wreaking too much havoc. As lions became deadlier, so gazelles evolved to run faster, hyenas to cooperate better, and rhinoceroses to be more bad-tempered. In contrast, humankind ascended to the top so quickly that the ecosystem was not given time to adjust. Moreover, humans themselves failed to adjust. Most top predators of the planet are majestic creatures. Millions of years of dominion have filled them with self-confidence. *Sapiens*, by contrast, is more like a banana republic dictator. Having so recently been one of the underdogs of the savannah, we are full of fears and anxieties over our position, which makes us doubly cruel and dangerous. Many historical calamities, from deadly wars to ecological catastrophes, have resulted from this over-hasty jump (Harari 2015).

The simplistic view that science has proven the universe is void of consciousness, magic, and wonder is part of modern man's hubris. Perhaps humans are not the top dog and host to the highest intelligence in the universe or even on Earth. The idea that greater wisdom is available to our psyches through psychedelic medicines is fundamental to my work as a psychedelic therapist. We wrongly assume what we know at any given time is the limit to the complexity of the universe. Curiosity and openness are fruitful and edifying as we navigate this incredible world. We each have the unique opportunity, perhaps a duty, to witness this grand unfolding with a sense of wonder and awe.

SECTION TWO

3
THE PSYCHEDELIC LANDSCAPE

How can we conceive of the validity and value of the realms of imagination? Recounting psychedelic experiences through storytelling, visual art, poetry, writing, dance, and other forms of creative expression are all ways we attune to the imaginal realm and create material manifestations of our interpretation of it. I have often wondered if experiences in psychedelic journeys offer a direct line to the collective unconscious and the imaginal realms. These fundamental conundrums about what exactly constitutes the collective unconscious are not settled issues. We are still grappling with where and what consciousness is and from where it emanates. Art, psychology, and psychedelics provide ways of exploring these questions and bringing material back to our shared reality.

The Invention of Discovery and the Discovery of Invention: Art, Psychology, and Psychedelics

Before becoming a therapist, I was a trained visual artist. Creating art is much like the psychedelic experience. Both are explorations of consciousness and finding where one's creativity merges with the collective imagination. When making the object of art, a fundamental point of triangulation is created for the artist/dreamer and viewer/witness to reflect upon together. The dyad becomes a triad. A landmark is placed on the psychic map and remains a reference point. As the artist records images and the feelings they elicit, a preverbal nostalgia and sentiment are evoked. I once painted a series of works based on what I saw in my dreamscapes; more gifts from my psyche were the reward. Being witnessed and appreciated, my unconscious brought more material from the imaginal realm and into the light of day through my artistic expression.

My thesis in counseling psychology at Pacifica Graduate Institute explored dream analysis, painting, and the Hero's Journey. I have been delighted to find that psychedelic journeys parallel the art-making process in many symbolic ways. There is a realm that is full of archetypal and imaginal forms. Through the ages, philosophers and artists have called these by different names. Plato (c. 427 – c. 347 BCE) understood there was an ideal dimension that informs the actual world. He asserts that we understand the phenomena of our world by contemplating them in their ideal forms or abstract essences. The Platonic Forms belong to an ideal dimension, and anything created in the material realm is a secondhand, less perfect version of the ideal. The Neoplatonists furthered the concept by developing three fundamental principles: the One, the Intellect, and the Soul. Platonism is a method of abstracting the finite world of humans, animals, and objects from the infinite world of the Ideal or the One. Neoplatonism, on the other hand, seeks to locate the One, or God in Christian Neoplatonism, in the finite world and human experience.

When Michelangelo was asked how he created his beautiful sculptures, he answered that they preexisted inside the marble. He was merely liberating them from the stone. Although debated by scholars, a quote attributed to Michelangelo is, "The sculpture is already complete within the marble block before I start my work. It is already there; I just have to chisel away the superfluous material." Everything other than the ideal form is Michelangelo's "superfluous material."

Much later, C.G. Jung developed the concept of the archetypal realm, where archetypal beings live through us in the physical world by influencing the formation of our rituals, symbols, emotions, behaviors, imaginations, perceptions, ideas, and choices. James Hillman and Henry Corbin, as Jungians, developed the concept of the imaginal realm. Archetypal psychologist James Hillman asserts that the world is patterned upon the template of the imaginal realm. Hillman argues a preexisting imaginal realm exists, and we may open our apertures of perception through various practices. We can tune our awareness to receive information awaiting us and transcribe insights from the imaginal into the material world through communication and artistic self-expression:

> What else is there besides the art product, the patient, and the emotion? Imagination. Since art therapy activates imagination and allows it to materialize—that is, enter the world via the emotions of the patient—therapy by means of the arts must take precedence over all other kinds (Hillman 1960).

Artistic expression, dream recollection, storytelling, and the integration of psychedelic material by psychotherapeutic processing offer shared awareness by creating evocative expressions. The therapeutic value of art and creativity has similar value when creative insights are shared about the psychedelic experience. This process provides a labyrinth within the personal psyche for us to navigate as we make the image, write and speak the words, or reflect upon the "dream" during its production. This process ushers in another phase of the creative process. Witnessing the words, sounds, movements, and art constellates material in the psyche of each witness. There is an additional component of creating a symbol of activation to invite and empower others to record their own subtle experiences with the imaginal realm. Artists often need their work to be witnessed and mirrored by others. Self psychologist Ernest Wolf talked about the need for mirroring:

> Creative people frequently depend on the presence of some other person or persons—or, sometimes, some object that symbolized the presence of the other—for the exercise of their creative skills and talents (Wolf 1988, 4).

The artistic process follows a similar trajectory to the psychotherapeutic process. The art creation experience is circular. The libidinal drive to create something is the first stage, followed by forging the vision into something tangible. The next phase involves bringing the creation into the public arena for witnessing. Next are the feedback, critiques, and inspiration received in response to the shared creation. Finally, that energy can be channeled into more fuel for the libidinal creative fire to make more art. The path is made through the very act of walking it, and the creative process is affirmed by listening, creating, sharing, and witnessing. In the therapeutic process, the psychedelic journey sparks a connection to the imaginal realms. The journeyer relays the experience while the therapist witnesses it. The therapist validates the experience, which helps the journeyer integrate and make sense of the journey and weave it into meaning for daily life. In psychology, integration refers to the process of combining different aspects of one's personality or self-concept into a unified whole. This can involve integrating different parts of one's identity, such as cultural or personal values, beliefs, and experiences, into a coherent sense of self. Integration can also refer to the process of integrating different aspects of one's emotions, thoughts, and behaviors into a unified whole.

Integration is an essential concept in psychedelic-assisted psychotherapy. It refers to making meaning from the symbolic content of the journey and applying these insights to daily life. An example of how raw symbolic imagery can be used to integrate difficult psychological material is seen in Frida Kahlo's paintings. I found her work raw and highly personal when I first saw it. Self-portraits, soaking in a bathtub with sores on her feet, milk dripping from her breasts, crying. Initially, I was embarrassed by it. I felt I was looking into her secret world to which I shouldn't be privy. However, I began appreciating her generosity as I sat with her paintings. She had fearlessly created a landmark for the fleeting imagery of her archetypal dreamscape. She brought these visions out of her depths, meticulously painting, hour after hour, images of her suffering, then laid them out bare-breasted for the world to see. By giving concrete imagery to her interior world, Kahlo not only encourages the viewer to feel their suffering but also validates the documentation of those feelings. She beckons the witness to remember how we all suffer in the human condition. We are not alone in our struggle, and Joseph Campbell recognized this too. "Artists are magical helpers. Evoking symbols and motifs that connect us to our deeper selves, they can help us along the heroic journey of our own lives" (Campbell 2004). This intimacy is similar to being a therapist and listening to deeply personal stories.

Art taps into the sublime experience. It is open-ended for interpretation, much like the original content of a dream. Every time we look at a painting, read a poem, or listen to a song, the experience reverberates with whatever else the witness is experiencing at that point in time. Each time is new to us; we never step into the same river twice. Poems, dance, and music are similar in this way. At my retreats, I offer markers, paints, and large sheets of paper for participants to record their experiences while they are still partly in the imaginal realm and before they coagulate their journeys into concrete stories. Linguist Benny Shanon articulates the power of ayahuasca to provide access to the collective unconscious and the potential of human creativity:

Along with language of the use of tools, art and creation are key defining features of what it is to be a member of the species *Homo sapiens*. In other words, human beings have—as a species—been made to develop art and music, seek the transcendent, and worship the holy. None of these accomplishments were there the day *Homo sapiens* first appeared on the stage of this planet. But were anyone to look at the species from a larger time perspective, perhaps from the perspective of the eternal, it would appear that human beings were made precisely in this fashion—to create the very specific things that they have actually created in the course of history— palaces and temples, paintings and sculptures, scientific theories, and metaphysical ideas. What Ayahuasca seems to be doing is to let time pass exceedingly fast and to let the mind be creative to the utmost. When the cognitive capacities of the individual are thus heightened and when the temporal constraints are greatly reduced, individuals may create, spontaneously and without apparent effort what, in the actual course of history, it has taken entire cultures countless generations to accomplish (Shanon 2002, 399).

Once in a while, I will have a psychedelic journey so incredibly profound that I can't help but believe other realities exist; they exist and function whether or not I am there to witness them. Sentient beings are going on with their lives, suddenly noticing and taking a sincere interest in me. Psychedelic visions contain creatures beckoning and celebrating my arrival. There is no way my brain could fabricate this. I must be discovering another plane of reality that exists independently. The creativity in these spaces is so complex and overwhelming that it is difficult to imagine a single human could produce its splendor.

If the doors of perception were cleansed, everything would appear to man as it is, infinite. For man has closed himself up, till he sees all things thro' narrow chinks of his cavern.

—WILLIAM BLAKE

A painting my husband, Martin Stensaas, and I created together in 2021 called *The Invention of Discovery* is based on psychedelic trips and the exploration of whether we are discovering a reality "out there" outside personal perception. Or are we inventing an elaborate reality from our unconscious of everything seen and stored in our minds? Like the AI program, Midjourney, accepts word prompts to create a unique image, maybe psychedelics scrape internal brain data for every image, sound, and emotion we've ever experienced. This data constructs a fantasy so immersive that it's hard to believe one person could create such an ornate dream world.

Are journeyers discovering a world or inventing it? The imaginal world may exist as a template behind the material one. I was told once by an ayahuascero apprentice that his mentor, the medicine man, would go into the ayahuasca space and place items, akin to an Easter egg hunt, for the students to find in subsequent journeys. If the apprentice was skilled enough to navigate the ayahuasca realm and find the objects, they were allowed to progress to the next lesson. This story fascinates me because it suggests that journeyers travel to an actual, alternative reality that we can independently verify. Journeyers have shared many stories with me over the years as they emerge from the "other side." These involve archetypes, the beings encountered, and landscapes that are frequently consistent from person to person. Although evidence and independent verification is lacking, there are many anecdotes of people having similar details of shared experience.

The Antipodes of the Mind: Charting the Phenomenology of the Ayahuasca Experience by Benny Shanon (2022) catalogs the full extent of the ayahuasca phenomena in Central and South America. In reflecting upon whether everything experienced in the psychedelic journey is invented or discovered, he asserts that, with ayahuasca, there is a collaboration and synthesis between the imaginal and the material realms. We are discovering an immensely powerful expanded psyche we can access with these medicines. His thesis is that the psyche is incredibly potent, and everyday waking reality cannot access its full power.

Especially related to our discussion is still another domain in which similar considerations may apply—that of myth. Do universals in myths reflect only commonalities in the conditions of the life of human beings, their psychological make-ups, and the structure and mode of functioning of their minds? Can myths be fully accounted for in empiricist terms? Can they be explained in terms that are strictly psychological and individualistic? Or perhaps, as in the case of language and music, some aspects of myth be accounted for in such terms? ... As for the fourth dimension mentioned above, myth, it may very well be the case that the problems presented by it are identical to those presented by Ayahuasca. In both cases, the commonalities involve specific contents. It may also be the case that the two are causally, not only conceptually, linked. If myths were discovered by their originators through the use of substance–induced altered states of consciousness, then the world of myth is actually the world of ayahuasca. I tend to believe that this is indeed the case (Shanon 2022, 395).

Research shows that psychedelics positively affect neuronal networks in the brain and neurochemistry to cure mental illness. Exploring our consciousness and alternate realities for exploration and self-awareness is also worthwhile. The value of psychedelic therapy is found in the experiences and in the exploration of a stimulated imagination and making meaning from it. This can give us hope and a sense of expanding possibilities.

Psychedelics and Psychotherapy

I am an advocate for the sovereignty of individual consciousness. Humans should have the right to do whatever they want to their own minds. Plant medicines must become decriminalized, legal, and available to anyone who wants to use them for noble purposes. I do not support the idea that we need to control access to plant medicines and punish people who use them with legal consequences. In saying this, we must also be aware of the ability of psychedelics to awaken people to their own empowerment and sovereignty of their consciousness and will. Conventional human power structures like religions and governments are often uneasy in the face of potent changing agents like psychedelics. The process of psychedelics going mainstream could make hierarchical organizations come under epistemic scrutiny, and their claims to power and legitimacy appear absurd.

There is a political dimension to the often-radical accountability and insights that psychedelic experiences often occasion. American psychologist and neuroscientist Dr. Carl Hart argues that current drug policies are based on misinformation and stereotypes of drug users. Misguided efforts have criminalized large population segments, such as socioeconomically disadvantaged and BIPOC populations. Hart calls for a paradigm shift from criminalizing drug use to a more compassionate and evidence-based approach. He advocates a system that treats drug addiction as a medical condition rather than a moral failing. In *Drug Use for Grown-Ups: Chasing Liberty in the Land of Fear* (2021), Dr. Hart argues that the current approach causes more harm than good. He advocates for decriminalization and the safe use of drugs for adults, sometimes with medical supervision. He asserts this type of drug policy would be more beneficial in creating peace.

While psychedelics can produce incredible insights and awakenings without the support of a therapist, research shows that healing outcomes are optimized when psychedelics are combined with psychotherapy by a well-trained mental health clinician. The consensus among many psychedelic researchers and therapists is the recommendation that the psychotherapist be aware of the set, setting, dose, and frequency when creating a treatment plan for each patient. It is a collaborative effort between psychedelic medicines and psychotherapy. When preparation, support, and integration harmonize, the potency and effectiveness of the treatment are greatly enhanced.

The range of sensory and cognitive changes can be broad within each psychedelic agent. Each psychedelic medicine has its own signature, but many have overlapping qualities. The following section covers each psychedelic medicine and its history, duration, and range of effects.

Medicines, History, and Dosage

Every psychedelic medicine has its "signature," which refers to the unique qualities inherent to the substance, its duration, and its physical, emotional, and spiritual effects. Although psychedelics have a wide range of effect phenomena, the character of each specific medicine can have distinct qualities. Scientifically oriented people focus on the signature to mean the duration, dosage, psychological and physical effects, and which receptor system(s) the drug binds to in the brain. They also concentrate on the physiological and psychological benefits.

Many indigenous and spiritually oriented people assert that each plant medicine has these effects and a unique spiritual essence. Ayahuasca, peyote, iboga, and psilocybin are all referred to as "plant medicines" and come from a lineage of indigenous people of the Americas, Africa, Europe, and Asia. If you plan to develop a relationship with sacred plants used traditionally in indigenous cultures, learn the traditions, preferably directly from indigenous people who continue the traditions of peyote, ayahuasca, psilocybin, and other new-world medicines. Learn about iboga and its practices from West African medicine people. Show respect and humility and understand the long-held traditions of each culture. As we deepen our understanding of "best practices," we learn the wisdom and benefits of indigenous cultural practices developed over centuries or millennia.

Western chemists developed ketamine, LSD, mescaline, DMT, and MDMA in the twentieth century. The more recent twentieth-century psychedelic traditions from the 1950s onward have much wisdom to offer as we continue to develop best practices for synthetic psychedelic medicines for therapeutic uses.

What follows is an overview of the most common psychedelics. While not intended to be an exhaustive exploration, it is a basic summary of their history, effects, and research status.

Ketamine

I was asked in a podcast interview, "When all the other psychedelics are legalized, Sunny, will you still offer ketamine therapy?" That is an enthusiastic *YES!* for several reasons. Ketamine is a flexible medicine. It behaves almost like a different drug at various doses and routes of administration. It is remarkably safe at low and moderate doses, has few interactions with other medications, and has more predictable effects than other psychedelics. Ketamine allows for extraordinary creativity and flexibility in treatment planning due to its different qualities at different dosages. It is also very sustainable for therapists and patients regarding time commitment. Importantly for many patients, ketamine enables people to remain on psychotropic medications because of its receptor profile, unlike other serotonergic-based classic psychedelics.

The organic chemist Calvin Stevens synthesized ketamine in 1962. The U.S. Food and Drug Administration (FDA) approved it for human use in 1970. It is still commonly used as an anesthetic and is on the World Health Organization Model List of Essential Medicines and is on the World Health Organization Model List of Essential Medicines. (WHO, 2021) Studies have looked at ketamine's ability to ease treatment-resistant depression. A study at Yale recognized that ketamine produces glutamate in the brain, stimulating new neural connections (Krystal et al. 2019). An explosion of research that followed has repeatedly confirmed ketamine's potential to resolve destructive mental patterning in depression and other mental health conditions at least in part through stimulation of new neural connections. Previous studies found that depressed people have abnormalities in their brains' glutamatergic systems. Overactive glutamate receptors result in depression, and ketamine blocks glutamatergic receptors.

Low-dose ketamine, referred to as a "psycholytic dose," allows clients to engage and talk throughout the session while in a trance-like state. Medium doses relax the body while the mind is in a psychedelic state. Often mystical experiences occur at these doses. High doses are used for anesthesia, and there is little to no retention of the visionary or emotional content.

A signature characteristic unique to ketamine is the sensation of the "spirit body" moving, flying, swimming, being turned, and being stretched. Psychedelic hallucinations can be fractal, machine-like, less common, earthy, and natural. It is common for travelers to watch prior memories unfold with detachment as if they are in what I call the "observer's mind." This experience offers much potential therapeutic value for therapists. Clients may use this "observer" witnessing to obtain some distance from traumatic memories.

There are several routes of administration. Ketamine can be insufflated as a powder or inhaled through a nebulizer inhaler. It may be given as a liquid or oral lozenge. It may be injected into a muscle, or it may be administered by intravenous drip. Each route of administration has a unique bioavailability and absorption, duration, and propensity for nausea and other side effects. About five percent of patients experience nausea with orally administered ketamine. It is less common with intramuscular injection, but nausea can still occur. This unfortunate side effect usually happens as patients begin to emerge out of the ketamine journey. Many practitioners use anti-nausea medication prophylactically to prevent this discomfort.

Depression is known to cause inflammation in the body, and ketamine has anti-inflammatory effects. It is a powerful antidote to anxiety, particularly social anxiety. It is often used off-label to treat PTSD and complex PTSD, frequently comorbid with anxiety and depression.

Ketamine affects various brain regions, including the medial prefrontal cortex in the frontal lobe. The medial prefrontal cortex is where emotions are regulated. The amygdala acts like a smoke detector in the brain, particularly the right amygdala. It senses danger and controls decision-making, determining punishment versus reward, memory, and emotional responses. Ketamine decreases the primacy of the right amygdala. Also affected are the periaqueductal gray and the anterior cingulate cortex. These brain regions control chronic pain, some autonomic functions, attention allocation, morality, ethics, reward anticipation and impulse control, decision-making, emotion, and understanding of physical pain. The hippocampus is also affected by ketamine, consolidating memories, spatial orientation, navigation, emotion, and learning. Ketamine also affects the nucleus accumbens, where aversion, reward, interpretation of motivation, reinforcement learning, and the brain's interpretation and reaction to addiction occur.

Salvia Divinorum

Salvia divinorum, also known as "ska María Pastora" or "Diviner's Sage," is a plant species native to Mexico. Salvia has a lesser-known but long history in traditional indigenous healing practices. It contains the psychoactive compound salvinorin A, responsible for the plant's characteristic, powerful hallucinogenic effects. The duration of the effects of *Salvia divinorum* varies depending on the dose and the method of administration but typically lasts five to thirty minutes. When smoked, the acute phase lasts five to ten minutes. When the leaves are chewed orally in a "quid" (used like chewing tobacco and placed in the mouth, usually between the gum and cheek), the effects are generally milder and last thirty to sixty minutes.

There is growing interest in the potential therapeutic benefits of *Salvia divinorum*. Some preliminary studies have suggested that it may treat addiction, depression, and chronic pain. Salvinorin A is a highly selective kappa-opioid receptor agonist, which may account for its unique therapeutic properties. The effects of *Salvia divinorum* can be intense and include changes in perception, such as visual and auditory hallucinations, and altered thought patterns and emotions. The experience is often described as dreamlike or out-of-body and can be disorienting. Due to the short duration of the effects, *Salvia divinorum* is considered a "dimethyltryptamine (DMT)-like" experience, but it differs from DMT as it is not a classic serotonergic psychedelic. It can feel similar to ketamine but with sharper imagery.

We don't understand the exact mechanisms of *Salvia divinorum* in the brain. It's important to note the kappa-opioid receptor is different from other opioid receptors and is not involved in addiction and the adverse side effects of classic opioids. In fact, salvia shows promise for treating opiate addiction. Despite its increasing popularity, research on *Salvia divinorum* is still in the early stages, and more research is needed to fully understand its effects and potential therapeutic uses. However, studies have shown it is nonaddictive, nontoxic, and non-habit-forming.

MDMA (2CB, etc.)

MDMA, 3,4-Methylenedioxymethamphetamine, can be found in a cream-colored powder, tablet, or crystal form. MDMA isn't considered a psychedelic but rather a potent empathogen–entactogen with stimulant properties. The desired effects include altered sensations, increased energy, empathy, and sensual pleasure. MDMA was first synthesized in 1912 by the German pharmaceutical company Merck and rediscovered by chemist Sasha Shulgin in 1965.

Shulgin created many chemical analogs to MDMA, including 2CB, 2CE, MDA, Aleph I, DIPT, and 5-MEO-DIPT, also known as foxy methoxy. Each of these compounds has a different signature. You can learn more about these chemicals in Sasha and Ann Shulgin's book, *TiHKAL: The Continuation* (1997). This book is a sequel to *PiHKAL: A Chemical Love Story* and explores the family of psychoactive drugs known as tryptamines. TiHKAL is an acronym for "Tryptamines I Have Known and Loved."

Therapists adopted MDMA early on as a powerful therapeutic aid in marital therapy. Sasha Shulgin's wife, Ann, was a prominent couples therapist who used MDMA extensively to heal relationships. Later, MDMA became popular at dance parties and was rebranded as "ecstasy." Ecstasy inspired the rave culture in the early 1980s, and the U.S. government designated MDMA as a Schedule I illegal drug in 1984.

The Multidisciplinary Association for Psychedelic Studies (MAPS) is a North American nonprofit organization working to raise awareness and understanding of MDMA and other psychedelic substances. The association was founded in 1986 by Rick Doblin and has raised millions of dollars privately to fund research. MAPS focuses on legalizing and rescheduling MDMA as a prescription drug to be administered by licensed healthcare clinicians and accompanied by two certified therapists trained at MAPS. As of 2023, MDMA is in Expanded Access status in treatment for PTSD. Experts expect MDMA to be legal for prescription use with approved and adequately trained therapists by 2024.

Psilocybin

Psilocybin is a classic psychedelic that binds to 5-HT2A receptors. It is a naturally occurring compound found in over 200 species of mushrooms all over the Americas, Europe, and Asia. These fungi are commonly referred to as "magic mushrooms." The primary effects of psilocybin include visual and auditory hallucinations and changes in perception of time and space. The duration of the effects of psilocybin can vary but typically lasts between four and six hours. Psychedelic therapists are in therapy with clients for ten hours from the beginning to the end of the session.

Recent research has suggested that psilocybin has therapeutic benefits for several mental health conditions, including depression, anxiety, and PTSD. A 2020 meta-analysis published in the *Journal of Psychopharmacology* found that psilocybin-assisted therapy was associated with "large and clinically significant" reductions in symptoms of depression and anxiety. Another study published in 2021 in *The New England Journal of Medicine* found that psilocybin therapy effectively reduced depression and anxiety in patients with life-threatening cancer (Carhart-Harris et al. 2021).

Despite the potential therapeutic benefits of psilocybin, the compound is currently illegal in most countries outside of FDA-approved research studies. However, in recent years there has been a growing movement to decriminalize the possession and use of psilocybin. Cities such as Denver, Oakland, and Santa Cruz, and states such as Colorado and California, have passed laws to decriminalize the possession and use of magic mushrooms.

Psilocybin journeys can produce laughter, "ego dissolution," and overcoming the fear of death in some. It is nearly impossible to overdose on psilocybin. It has low addiction potential and has been shown to reduce depression, even at microdose levels. That's not to say challenging journeys are uncommon or unlikely. Though effects may vary, psilocybin can create delightful feelings of connection, playfulness, and insight into one's life and our place in the cosmos. A sense of deep connection to others, love, and compassion toward nature are common afterglow experiences.

Psilocybin has been used for thousands of years by indigenous people. The Mazatec culture in Mexico has a long tradition of sacred psilocybin use. The use of hallucinogenic mushrooms in Mesoamerica has been documented thanks to the discovery of "mushroom stones," small sculptures resembling a mushroom. According to a paper by Elisa Guerra-Doce, the sculptures have been found at numerous sites dating back to 500 BC and AD 900 in Guatemala, Mexico, Honduras, and El Salvador. Psychedelic mushrooms may have been used in Africa and Europe as well. Mushroom-looking pictographs in the prehistoric mural paintings at Villar del Humo in Cuenca, Spain may represent hallucinogenic mushrooms. Mushroom-shaped carvings in rocky outcrops dating from the Neolithic and Bronze Ages in northwest Piedmont, in the Italian Alps, have been interpreted as signs of ritual psychotropic mushroom use. In *Food of the Gods: The Search for the Original Tree of Knowledge*, Terence McKenna explores the idea that the consumption of psychoactive plants like psilocybin played a significant creativity-inducing role in developing human consciousness, culture, and spirituality. He argues that these substances led to the evolution of language, religion, and art.

Most accounts credit R. Gordon Wasson for discovering psilocybin mushrooms and bringing them to the United States. But Wasson's wife, Valentina Pavlovna Guercken, first introduced him to hallucinogenic mushrooms. In 1927, on their honeymoon in New York's Catskill Mountains, Valentina found mushrooms similar to the ones she had known in her native Russia. This discovery sparked the couple's interest, and they studied and incorporated mycology with other disciplines, such as religion, art, history, and linguistics. In 1953, Wasson and his wife led expeditions to Mexico to research the religious use of mushrooms by the native people. The Wassons were the first Westerners to witness a mushroom *velada* (ceremony) and, during a later visit, participate in a *velada* led by local healer Maria Sabina. Sabina was hesitant to reveal the mushroom ceremony to the Wassons and later came to regret it. In a 1957 article in *LIFE* magazine, Wasson coined the term "magic mushroom" (1957, May 13). The article detailed his experiences and resulted in hordes of North Americans traveling to the tiny town of Huautla de Jiménez, Mexico, searching for magic mushrooms. The community eventually shunned Maria Sabina for revealing the secrets of the mushrooms and attracting unwanted visitors. Local villagers burned Sabina's house to the ground, and she died extremely poor and malnourished.

Over the years, Wasson and botanist Roger Heim collected and identified several species of mushrooms and sent samples to the chemist Albert Hofmann who worked at Sandoz Laboratories in Switzerland and was the first person to synthesize LSD. Using this material, Hofmann isolated and identified the compounds psilocybin and psilocin. Interestingly, in all research studies in the U.S., only the extract of psilocin is used, rather than the entire fungus, because the FDA hasn't approved all of the constituents of the mushroom fruiting body. Therefore, only the psychedelic-synthesized chemical is used for FDA-approved studies.

On October 27, 1970, the U.S. government classified psilocybin and psilocin as Schedule I drugs. They were simultaneously labeled "hallucinogens" under a section of the Comprehensive Drug Abuse Prevention and Control Act, known as the Controlled Substances Act.

Psilocybin continued to inspire mycologists, scientists, and those interested in consciousness and mystical experiences. Amateur scientist and mycologist Paul Stamets has been a significant influence in the resurgence of psilocybin. His research has contributed immensely to the psychedelic and mycology fields.

Psilocybin rewires the brain for people suffering from depression. According to a study by scientists at UC San Francisco and Imperial College London (Daws et al. 2022), psilocybin fosters significant connections between different brain regions in depressed people, freeing them up from long-held patterns of rumination and excessive self-focus. Scientists analyzed fMRI brain scans of nearly sixty participants in two psilocybin trials. In the first analysis, all the participants had treatment-resistant depression and knew they were given psilocybin. In the second one, the participants were depressed but not as severely, and researchers did not tell them whether they had been given psilocybin or a placebo, escitalopram, which is an SSRI antidepressant. In addition to the drugs, all the participants received the same type of psychotherapy. The scans before and after treatment showed the psilocybin treatment reduced connections within brain areas tightly connected in depression, including the default mode, salience, and executive networks. The psilocybin increased connections to other brain regions that were not well integrated. Participants were also less emotionally avoidant, and their cognitive functioning improved. The improvement in their depressive symptoms correlated with changes in their brains, and these changes lasted three weeks after the second psilocybin dose. No such changes were seen in the brains of those who received escitalopram. Psilocybin acts differently on the brain than SSRIs.

Psilocybin and other serotonergic psychedelics like ayahuasca affect 5-HT2A receptors, plentiful in brain networks that become overactive in depression. One hypothesis is that the drugs briefly disrupt these connections, allowing them to re-form in new ways in the ensuing days and weeks. "For the first time, we find that psilocybin works differently from conventional antidepressants – making the brain more flexible and fluid and less entrenched in the negative thinking patterns associated with depression," said David Nutt, DM, head of the Imperial Centre for Psychedelic Research. "This supports our initial predictions and confirms psilocybin could be a real alternative approach to depression treatments" (Kurtzman 2022).

LSD

LSD creates mental, visual, and auditory hallucinations. It dilates the pupils and increases blood pressure, with effects lasting up to twenty hours, although twelve hours is typical. LSD is also capable of causing profound mystical experiences and is known for its ability to initiate "ego dissolution." LSD is the typical "classical" psychedelic, primarily because it is an agonist of the brain's 5-HT2A (serotonin) receptor. LSD also binds to dopamine receptors, which is why it tends to be more stimulating than psilocybin. An intriguing fact about LSD is that the molecule's interesting structure serves as a manhole cover. When it binds to the 5-HT2A receptor site, it pulls a "lid" over itself to burrow into the receptor. Chemists believe this is why LSD requires such a small dose and has an extraordinarily long duration of effect.

LSD is typically taken orally and sold on blotter paper or in liquid form. It is considered nonaddictive, with a low potential for abuse. LSD is active in minimal amounts relative to other psychoactive compounds, and doses are measured in micrograms. Toxic overdose from LSD has never been documented, and if taken frequently, tolerance develops quickly, reducing its effects.

In 1938, Swiss chemist Albert Hofmann first synthesized LSD from lysergic acid, a chemical derived from ergot, a fungus that infects grain. Hofmann discovered its psychedelic effects in 1943 after unintentionally ingesting an unknown amount, absorbing it through his skin. On April 19, celebrated since 1985 as Bicycle Day, Hofmann had his legendary bike ride home from his chemistry lab while on LSD. Interest in this fascinating molecule spread throughout Europe and North America. Humphry Osmond began LSD-assisted psychotherapy in the 1950s and 1960s. Psychotherapists used LSD to treat alcoholism and other mental illnesses with promising results. During this time, the CIA began using LSD in Project MKUltra, which utilized psychoactive substances to aid in interrogation. The CIA illegally administered LSD to unwitting test subjects to observe how they would react. The truth about Project MKUltra was hidden from the public for years.

Dr. Stanislav Grof also began working with LSD. Grof is known in scientific circles for his early studies of LSD and its psychological effects. In the 1960s, LSD and other psychedelics were adopted by the counterculture movement and the hippies. These substances were considered a cultural threat to American values and the Vietnam War. LSD was listed as a Schedule I controlled substance by the United Nations in 1971. The use of LSD among U.S. adults increased by 56.4 percent from 2015 to 2018.

Today, less research is conducted on LSD than on psilocybin, MDMA, and ketamine, but LSD shows much potential in treating mental illness and improving wellness and creativity.

Ayahuasca

Ayahuasca is a psychedelic brew made from the ayahuasca vine (*Banisteriopsis caapi*) and the leaves of the chacruna plant (*Psychotria viridis*). The ayahuasca vine contains MAO inhibitors, which prevent the breakdown of certain neurotransmitters and allow the psychoactive compounds in the chacruna leaves to produce intense hallucinations and a modified state of consciousness for several hours. The primary active ingredient in ayahuasca is dimethyltryptamine (DMT), a powerful psychedelic substance. The effects of ayahuasca typically last between four and six hours.

The indigenous people of the Amazon have been using the brew for centuries for spiritual ceremonies and healing purposes. In recent years, ayahuasca has spread beyond the Amazon region, becoming increasingly popular in Western countries as a personal growth and spiritual exploration tool. Fast-growing interest in ayahuasca has been both a boon and a problem, as its use has certain physical and psychological risks. The explosion in interest has also increased psychedelic tourism to small towns and villages in South America, which has been a mixed blessing. It has brought tourism money to local economies but has also created problems with the influx of North Americans and Europeans, including commercialization and exploitation of indigenous ceremonial practices. It has also attracted nonethical, self-appointed "shamans," some of whom are reported to have extorted money and sexually assaulted vulnerable ayahuasca tourists.

The effects of ayahuasca can be profound. They include visual and auditory hallucinations, warped perception of time and space, and intense bodily sensations. Additionally, many people who have taken ayahuasca report intense and cathartic emotional experiences and a profound sense of connection to nature and the universe. It is common, particularly after a series of ayahuasca experiences, to feel as if the trajectory of journeys takes the person through a "dark night of the soul" before they rise to resurrection and into mystical bliss. Reports of transcendence and spiritual awakening tell of life-changing insights.

Recent research has suggested that ayahuasca may have therapeutic benefits for various mental health conditions, including depression, anxiety, and PTSD. For example, a 2020 meta-analysis published in the *Journal of Psychoactive Drugs* found that ayahuasca-assisted therapy was associated with "large and clinically significant" reductions in symptoms of depression and anxiety (Luoma et al. 2020).

However, outside indigenous practices, ayahuasca is illegal in most countries. Furthermore, it is essential to note that ayahuasca can be dangerous if consumed in the wrong setting or with improper preparation. Ayahuasca consumption is best carried out under the guidance of a trained professional or an ethical and well-practiced indigenous ayahuascera/ayahuascero.

Ibogaine

A lesser-known psychedelic gaining interest is iboga, whose active compound is ibogaine. Iboga is found in shrubs indigenous to west Central Africa, mainly Gabon, Cameroon, and Congo. The shrub grows up to two meters in height, has yellow or pink flowers, and produces sweet, pulpy fruits without psychoactive alkaloids. The term "iboga" refers to many plants, including *Tabernanthe iboga, Tabernanthe manii, and Voacanga africana*, and is traditionally used in African cultures such as Bwiti. Traditionally, an enormous amount of root bark is consumed as a rite of passage, and smaller amounts are ingested for healing ceremonies. A typical therapeutic dose ranges from five to one hundred grams.

Iboga root bark causes nausea and vomiting—reactions associated with the iboga ritual—as opposed to its other forms. Some people contend that this purging is an essential spiritual component of the experience. Iboga is considered dangerous by Western scientists, who assert it has significant risks. Iboga can cause serious side effects such as heart problems, seizures, and hallucinations that can persist for days or weeks after use. It can also be toxic in large doses, and the plant's root bark has been associated with several deaths. Proper preparation beforehand, led by a knowledgeable and well-trained practitioner, and adhering to the preparation and ceremonial compliance, are essential.

Ibogaine, or ibogaine hydrochloride, is the name of the active compound in iboga. It can appear as off-white crystals or a clear liquid. Doses of fifteen to twenty milligrams per kilogram (as high as 1,400 milligrams for a 150-pound person) are typical. Many addiction treatment centers claim excellent results, especially with opiate addiction, as it can eliminate withdrawal symptoms. Ibogaine has been extracted and synthesized with ninety-nine-percent purity, so the dose can be carefully controlled and calibrated to suit a client's specific needs. Ibogaine passes through the system more quickly than iboga, clearing in about twenty-four hours. The journeys are often profoundly intense, with guidance from ancestors a common theme.

5-MeO-DMT

5-methoxy-N, N-dimethyltryptamine (5-MeO-DMT) is a powerful psychedelic that can be made synthetically and found in the venom of the Bufo toad, also known as the Colorado River toad. The compound is known for its powerful hallucinogenic effects, which are similar to those of other psychedelic substances. It is structurally similar to other psychedelics, such as DMT and psilocybin, but is considered significantly more potent. When smoked, the effects of 5-MeO-DMT typically last between thirty and sixty minutes.

The discovery of DMT is credited to Hungarian chemist Dr. Stephen Szára, who first synthesized the compound in 1956. However, indigenous Amazonian cultures had used ayahuasca, a brew containing DMT, for centuries before its formal discovery. DMT is found naturally in several plants, including the ayahuasca vine, and has been used for religious and medicinal purposes in various cultures around the world.

While the Bufo toad is a source of 5-MeO-DMT, the extraction process can be harmful to the toads and their habitats, leading to concerns about animal welfare and conservation. Using synthetic 5-MeO-DMT as an alternative can be more environmentally sustainable and humane. Moreover, synthetic production allows for greater purity and quality control, reducing the risk of contaminants or impurities that could be harmful to human health.

5-MeO-DMT needs more thorough documentation to understand its potential and history fully. In recent years, 5-MeO-DMT has become increasingly popular as a personal growth and spiritual exploration tool in Western countries. The effects of 5-MeO-DMT can be intense, including florid visual and auditory hallucinations and altered perception of time and space. Many people taking 5-MeO-DMT report having profound spiritual experiences, a sense of mystical transcendence, and merging with God, Goddess, or the Source. It also produces a powerful emotional experience that can profoundly impact the journeyer. Recent research has suggested that 5-MeO-DMT has therapeutic benefits for various mental health conditions, including depression, anxiety, PTSD, and addiction. A 2019 study published in the *Journal of Psychoactive Drugs* found that 5-MeO-DMT-assisted therapy significantly reduced symptoms of depression and anxiety (Davis et al. 2019). Another study published in the *Journal of Psychedelic Studies* in 2020 found that 5-MeO-DMT was effective in reducing symptoms of PTSD in veterans (Davis et al. 2020).

However, it is essential to note that 5-MeO-DMT is a powerful substance and should be used with caution. Its possession, distribution, and use are prohibited in most countries. Furthermore, it should only be consumed under the guidance of a trained professional, as the substance can be psychologically dangerous if consumed in the wrong setting or with improper preparation. The toads that produce 5-MeO-DMT are becoming endangered due to various factors, including habitat destruction and overharvesting by eager psychonauts. Protecting these species and their habitats is essential to preserve their ecological and cultural significance.

Mescaline/Peyote/Huachuma

Peyote is a small, spineless cactus that contains the psychoactive compound mescaline. The effects of peyote can vary depending on the dose and the individual but typically last six to twelve hours. Research on peyote is limited, but some evidence suggests it may have therapeutic potential for treating addiction, PTSD, and other mental illnesses. Mescaline, the active compound in peyote, is a phenethylamine and acts as a serotonin receptor agonist, which may account for its therapeutic effects.

The effects of peyote can be intense and mystical. They include changes in perception, producing immersive visual and auditory hallucinations, and changes in thoughts and emotions. Different areas of the brain become connected, and the experience is often described as dreamlike, mystical, or spiritual. Many people report feelings of euphoria, enhanced creativity, and increased empathy.

The exact mechanisms of peyote's action in the brain are not fully understood. However, mescaline is believed to act on the serotonin receptors, which regulate mood, cognition, and perception. Mescaline also acts as a 5-HT2A agonist.

Peyote has a long history of use in traditional indigenous healing practices, particularly among the Huichol, the Tarahumara, also known as the Rarámuri, and other indigenous tribes in Mexico. Peyote use in spiritual and ceremonial contexts is protected under the American Indian Religious Freedom Act of 1978. However, peyote is also a Schedule I controlled substance in the United States, which makes possession and distribution illegal for those using it outside of religious practices. The use of peyote is central to the religious practices of the Native American Church, which has an estimated 250,000 members.

The cactus is harvested in the wild. However, due to overharvesting and habitat destruction, wild populations of peyote are becoming increasingly rare. Overharvesting is causing concern for conservationists working to protect the cactus, its habitat, and indigenous communities who use it for ceremonial practices. Efforts are being made to cultivate peyote sustainably, but this is a work in progress. Indigenous communities and environmental activists also advocate for expanding legal protection and recognition of the ceremonial use of peyote in traditional practices.

In contrast to endangered peyote, a ubiquitous natural psychedelic that contains mescaline is San Pedro, also known as "huachuma." Native to the Andean region of South America, it has been used for centuries by indigenous people for spiritual and medicinal purposes. The cactus contains several psychoactive compounds, the most prominent of which is mescaline. This psychedelic compound produces hallucinations, changes in perception, and altered states of consciousness.

Pharmacological studies have shown that mescaline acts primarily on the serotonin receptors in the brain, specifically the 5-HT2A receptor. The activation of this receptor is believed to be responsible for mescaline's psychedelic effects. Studies have also suggested that mescaline may have therapeutic potential for treating addiction, depression, and PTSD (Agin-Liebes et al. 2021). However, more research is needed to fully understand the mechanisms of mescaline action and the potential therapeutic benefits of San Pedro.

Lack of Standardized Psychedelic Therapy Methods

A standardized set of techniques or approved psychotherapeutic modalities do not exist in psychedelic-assisted psychotherapy due to the inability to streamline and quantify the qualitative, nuanced, and nonlinear nature of psychedelic experiences. Each psychedelic has its own signature, duration, and effects, so a singular universally approved therapeutic method for all psychedelic medicines seems unlikely.

However, there are essential core competencies for therapists preparing for, facilitating during, and integrating after psychedelic journeys. The safety and well-being of the patient are paramount. Psychedelic therapists must have adequate training in psychology and each specific psychedelic medicine's effects, duration, and contraindications. The journeyer's preparation and orientation are vital, as are safety and trust between the client and therapist. Therapists are encouraged to use a non-directive approach based on empathetic rapport and presence.

Proper training in trauma and processing complex material is essential, as are adequate time and therapeutic support to integrate the experience. Trauma inevitably emerges in the psychedelic space for people who have experienced trauma. In IFS terms, the manager and protector parts that usually push away the exiles who experienced the trauma from the conscious mind are downregulated during the psychedelic experience, allowing more access to those feelings (see Chapter Seven for a full discussion of the IFS model).

Attunement and empathetic, active listening are encouraged throughout the journey. Offering minimal overt verbal and nonverbal encouragement is also best practice. Therapists use words to invite rather than direct. They paraphrase and reflect on the journeyer's recounts to ensure they understand correctly. Therapists can assist the journeyer in understanding what they are feeling and connect emotion with bodily sensations and memories. Therapists can validate clients by offering reassurance and patience as the journeyer comes to apply their own meaning to the psychedelic experience.

This lack of a universal, standard therapeutic approach for psychedelics has a downside. Without a standardized therapeutic approach, capturing accurate, validated outcomes for psychedelic therapy is challenging. Additionally, without a baseline standard of care, there is potential for therapeutic modalities that are ineffective at best and dangerous at worst.

The MAPS MDMA training manual (2015) explains their approved therapy models as follows:

2.0 Therapist Foundation
…In addition to this specific training, it is required that participating therapists have a proper background, education, and experience as therapists. An important element of this background

experience with therapy for PTSD, which likely will include widely recognized therapies such as Prolonged Exposure (PE), Cognitive Processing (CPT), Eye Movement Desensitization and Reprocessing (EMDR), and psychodynamic psychotherapy. In addition, there are other less widely recognized approaches that offer valuable experience for MDMA researchers. These include Internal Family Systems (IFS), Voice Dialogue, Psychosynthesis, Hakomi, Sensorimotor Therapy, Holotropic Breathwork, Jungian psychology, Buddhist psychology, and Virtual Reality. Elements of each of these psychotherapeutic approaches may occur spontaneously in MDMA-assisted therapy.

At least by MAPS, it is understood that several therapeutic modalities are most beneficial when used with psychedelic medicine. EMDR, IFS, and Jungian psychology are all used in the Theradelic Approach, with the main emphasis on IFS.

The Need for Diverse Voices

Psychedelic medicine ceremonies originated and evolved in indigenous cultures through the local medicine women and men for centuries. Despite this history, the psychedelic professional landscape lacks enough representation from diverse populations such as BIPOC, LGBTQIA+, and women. The corporatization of plant-based psychedelics has led to extraction from the places and cultures where they originated.

This narrative glorifies Western science, consumerism, and capital investment and displaces indigenous healers who initially developed the knowledge around the uses of these medicines. The indigenous people shared plant medicines with Western scientists, who then extracted their knowledge and resources without reciprocity. The Western colonial science narrative is being pressured, however, and is hesitantly becoming more inclusive with marginalized groups insisting on fair representation. Despite this new awareness, a more significant shift is needed. The more diverse perspectives are added to the psychedelic renaissance, the more it will be influenced and informed to be multicultural, inclusive, and, frankly, better.

For several reasons, including diverse perspectives from people in psychedelic-assisted psychotherapy is crucial. First, doing so helps ensure that the therapy is culturally sensitive, inclusive, and accessible to a wide range of people, including those from marginalized communities. Secondly, incorporating diverse perspectives will result in a more nuanced and holistic understanding of the therapeutic healing of psychedelics and the potential risks or challenges. Finally, having a diverse team of therapists and researchers can help to address potential biases in study design and interpretation of results.

These medicinal practices produce the most robust positive results when offered in ways inclusive of mind, body, and spirit. There is an opportunity to connect the new science with respectful indigenous practices to generate reciprocity that benefits the people, animals, and plants where the uses of these medicines originated.

SECTION THREE

4
PRESUPPOSITIONS OF THE THERADELIC APPROACH

Let's take a deeper look at the foundations of the Theradelic Approach and the application of the method. Underlying all the presuppositions of the Theradelic Approach is a trust that we all have an inner voice that guides us toward wellness.

> *"For the greatest and most important problems of life,*
> *we must rely upon the inner strength of the human soul.*
> *Only that can help and bring us to a higher and more noble level.*
> *The most important thing is to be true to ourselves,*
> *to be true to our own inner voice.*
> *It is the only guide we can trust."*
>
> —C.G. JUNG

The Psyche has Inherent Wisdom

The psyche is inherently wise and will naturally move toward healing when provided with the conditions for wellness. Therapists must trust this process and provide interventions that lead to curiosity and insight. As therapists, we trust and support the client's biological and neurobiological systems.

As a psychotherapist, I imagine myself as a midwife of the psyche. What desires to be born from within each being will move along its natural path. My job as a psychotherapist is not to push, pull, or force change preemptively but rather to allow what is being born to arrive with as much ease and delight as possible. There is great joy in this process, and witnessing the birth of a client's potential is a sacred honor.

Humans Have Inherent Goodness

"You teach children they are valuable by treating them like they are, not by insisting that they prove their value to you."

—GREGORY BOYLE

As prosocial animals, humans are intrinsically good. Trauma, depression, anxiety, and mental illnesses can cover up that goodness. Humans naturally collaborate in moral, generous, and altruistic ways when given proper support and insight. This claim isn't a New Age spiritual bypass. Humans have evolved to cooperate and live in peaceful, collaborative societies. Prosocial behavior is hardwired in our DNA. The survival of the species is the survival of ourselves. Studies have shown that cooperation and altruism have been essential for the survival and success of human groups throughout history. For example, a survey by Gintis et al. (2003) found that cooperation and altruism were necessary for the evolution of human society, as these qualities allowed early humans to survive and thrive in challenging environments. Another study by Fehr and Fischbacher (2004) found that prosocial behavior is a universal human trait in all cultures and societies.

Additionally, research has shown that the neural mechanisms that underlie prosocial behavior are present in the brain from an early age. For instance, a study by Warneken and Tomasello (2006) found that even young children have an innate inclination to help others, which is evident in their prosocial behavior. Selfishness, competition, power, and greed are not intrinsic core qualities of human beings.

Observing children raised in an environment with consistent, secure attachment, void of traumatic events, demonstrates this. Watch any two-year-old child given consistent warmth and nurturing interactions with the world around them. Securely attached kids show a wonder about others and a desire to connect to them. They have developed a sense of trust and security in their primary caregivers, which allows them to explore their environment and form secure attachments. Studies have shown that securely attached children are more likely to seek out social interactions, approach and engage with unfamiliar people, and develop stronger relationships with their peers. Viewing it through an IFS lens, securely attached people exhibit more Self-led behavior—that is, experience compassion, calmness, confidence, and a sense of connection. A study by Cassidy and Shaver (1999) found that securely attached children were more likely to seek comfort and support from their caregivers during times of stress and had better social skills and more positive relationships with their peers. Another study by Waters and Cummings (2000) found that securely attached children were more likely to form strong, healthy relationships with others and less likely to experience social anxiety or social isolation. Unless there is neurological damage, trauma, neglect, or abuse, securely attached toddlers will smile, giggle, make eye contact, and approach others. Pain, isolation, instability, poverty, and experiences of cruelty warp a person's natural development of well-being and generosity.

A Nonpathological View of the Psyche

Therapists understand people do not consciously choose to be depressed, anxious, or traumatized. These conditions are not thinking errors but natural and creative adaptations from life experiences. Given our circumstances, our minds, bodies, and souls evolve perfectly and predictably. This presupposition liberates us from judgment and moves us toward acceptance, compassion, and discernment.

We understand the human psyche is complex, consisting of many personalities, archetypes, and what Dr. Richard Schwartz, the creator of IFS, has termed "parts." We negotiate with all these facets in therapy to create a healthy and whole internal ecosystem. Parts develop burdens when their roles become out of balance, extreme, and/or dissociated to deal with the strains and challenges of life events.

Different traditions recognize the central, wisest foundation of each of us as the Buddha, Christ Consciousness, the Great Mother, the Great Spirit, Divine Essence, and the Highest Self. In IFS, it is called the Self. IFS understands humans to be complex beings with multiple parts. All these facets of the personality evolve throughout life as we encounter other people and have experiences. Attachment dynamics are influenced by parts' development, the family we were born into, traumas, biology, neurobiology, relationships with friends, siblings, lovers, coworkers, etc. The manager and protector parts direct the system through controlling behaviors. Extreme protectors become firefighters—parts that desperately want to extinguish the pain of the exiles by dissociating the system from their suffering. The exiles are the most hurt parts who have been shunned and sent away. They are desperate to be witnessed and rescued. Behind all the parts is the timeless Self. The Self is calm, compassionate, confident, creative, caring, connected, curious, and clear. The Self does not have an agenda. Checking in to see if there is an agenda is a reliable way to sense if one is in Self energy.

IFS is a non-pathologizing approach in which the voices of different aspects of the personality are recognized and negotiated with to facilitate healing. IFS therapy aims to allow wise Self energy to shine through all parts. IFS is discussed in more depth in Chapter Seven.

Trauma Is in the Body; It Is Not a Thinking Error

Trauma is a nervous system response, not a thinking error. Fight, flight, freeze, and fawn are coping mechanisms of PTSD. We develop extreme, burdened parts as a response to trauma.

Simply talking about traumatic events does not heal trauma. The healing process is recognizing and releasing energy from the body, repatterning the nervous system and reactive responses, and creating compassion for oneself and all our parts developed in response to upsetting situations. Physician and addiction specialist Dr. Gabor Maté (2018) claims what causes most mental illnesses, addictions, and physical illnesses are traumatic events. We live in a society that tends to create trauma responses in the body. Socioeconomic and racial injustice, working long hours under stressful work conditions, long work days at a computer, and isolation from one another and the natural world can exacerbate trauma.

PTSD and trauma are not mere cognitive processes but rather nervous system responses to overwhelming experiences. Trauma is a normal emotional and physiological response to an event or situation perceived as life-threatening or overwhelming. When a person experiences trauma, the body's fight-or-flight response is activated, releasing a surge of stress hormones such as adrenaline and cortisol. These hormones prepare the body to respond to the threat by increasing heart rate, blood pressure, and respiration. This stress response should be turned off when the danger is over. However, in some people, the system remains activated, leading to chronic stress and the development of PTSD. The affected person is trapped in their traumatic memories, which haunt the victim and loop endlessly as if the trauma is still happening. This loop is separate from the executive command center and needs to be treated accordingly.

Research shows PTSD is a complex condition that involves changes in the nervous system, including alterations in the hypothalamic-pituitary-adrenal (HPA) axis, the sympathetic nervous system, and the immune system. Studies by Yehuda (2002) and Bremner (2002) found that people with PTSD have abnormal levels of stress hormones and changes in the structure and function of the hippocampus, a brain region involved in memory and emotion regulation. These changes can lead to various symptoms, including flashbacks, nightmares, anxiety, and depression, which can significantly negatively impact a person's life.

We Are Resilient and Can Grow Following Trauma

"We must be willing to get rid of the life we've planned
to have the life that is waiting for us.
The old skin has to be shed before the new one can come."

—JOSEPH CAMPBELL

We can heal after traumatic events. We are not our trauma. Nothing can make what has happened to us disappear, but we can find ways to be resilient and hopeful. We can unburden our terrified exiles and their extreme protectors. Therapists help clients develop a positive inner explanatory style by finding meaning in their lives. We find resilience and grit as we move from an external to an internal locus of control. We are hardwired to tell stories and to find patterns of meaning. Our prosocial behaviors are as intrinsic as our desire to make meaning through storytelling.

Psychological resilience and post-traumatic growth (PTG) refer to the ability to adapt and bounce back from adversity. Resilience is a multidimensional construct that includes personal and environmental factors contributing to a person's ability to cope with stress and adversity. Positive coping strategies, social support, and a sense of self-efficacy are all associated with psychological resilience.

Research has shown that PTG and psychological resilience are vital after traumatic events. PTG can be seen as a positive outcome of resilience. Research suggests that resilient people are more likely to experience growth as a result of their trauma. A study by Tedeschi and Calhoun (1996) found that people who reported higher levels of PTG also reported higher levels of resilience, which indicates the two are closely related.

We access the most wounded and hurt exiled parts of the internal ecosystem by utilizing IFS and psychedelic psychotherapy. With compassion, calmness, and curiosity from both the therapist and the client's Self, we support the psyche's natural inclination toward resiliency and growth.

Our Explanatory Styles and Loci of Control Can Help Us Heal

"There are two kinds of people in this world.
There are those who are dreamers, and those who are being dreamed.
There comes a time in every man's life when he must encounter his past.
For those who are dreamed, who have no more than a passing acquaintance with power,
this moment is usually played out from their deathbeds as they try to bargain
for a few more moments of lifetime. But for the dreamer, the person of power,
this moment takes place alone before a fire when he calls upon the specters
of his personal past to stand before him, like witnesses before the court.
This is the work of the Self, where the medicine wheel begins."

—ALBERTO VILLOLDO

Villoldo illustrates the importance of being the dreamer of one's life rather than being dreamed. The work of the Self and to become a person of power is telling one's life story as the dreamer. A positive explanatory style and an internal locus of control help us become resilient and develop a healthier sense of self and purpose. These factors affect the choices we make and the risks we take. In turn, these choices can lead to a more fulfilling life. This process creates the one who is dreaming their life into being. Effective psychedelic-assisted psychotherapy can help us detach from the traumas and negative experiences of the past and tell a new, more meaningful story. The story can empower us to escape from learned helplessness and repeating trauma patterns. Stories can renarrate trauma to support growth.

Dr. Martin Seligman is considered the father of positive psychology. Seligman developed explanatory style theory in 1954, which attempts to explain our tendency to offer similar explanations for different events. The term "explanatory style" describes how we explain the events of our lives. Our explanatory styles are the way we process events, attach meaning to those events, and assess whether they are threatening or challenging.

Self-talk and self-perception affect our stress levels in multiple ways. According to Seligman, there are three parameters for how people explain a situation to themselves and others: internality, stability, and globality. Internality is the belief that our successes or failures are primarily the results of our own actions and decisions rather than external factors beyond our control. Stability is the belief that an event or situation is unchanging and will remain consistent over time. Globality is the tendency to generalize a specific event or experience to all areas of one's life, leading to a broad and pervasive interpretation of oneself, others, and the world.

Each explanatory style can be either optimistic or pessimistic. The three styles are stable versus unstable (does it change or remain the same?), global versus local, and internal locus of control versus external locus of control. The locus of control refers to a person's belief about the source of control in their life, whether they believe they or something else maintains authority over their life's events.

People with an internal locus of control believe that they have control over the events in their lives and that their actions and decisions can influence the outcome. This belief is associated with positive outcomes such as high self-esteem, self-efficacy, and motivation. People with an internal locus of control tend to take responsibility for their actions and are more likely to persist when faced with failure. People with an external locus of control believe that external factors, such as luck, fate, or the actions of others, control the events in their lives. This belief is associated with characteristics such as low self-esteem, helplessness, and passivity. People with an external locus of control tend to blame external factors for their failures and may give up easily.

Learned helplessness is a condition in which one learns or assumes one's agency is futile. For example, someone repeatedly exposed to unavoidable painful or otherwise negative stimuli will create a pattern of expectation that such events cannot be influenced by their efforts. As a result, this pattern may establish a sense of hopelessness and depression (Overmier and Seligman 1967).

Through the IFS lens, each part has a positive or negative explanatory style. As parts are given the opportunity to process their pain and unburden, they naturally move out of learned helplessness and into resilience and empowerment. Watching for a distinctive shift in hopeful language helps the therapist track where the client is in the process of unburdening (unburdening is covered in more depth in Chapter Seven.)

We Follow Patterns and Cycles

I look past your words.
I don't even pay attention to your actions.
What I watch are your patterns.

Therapists understand the significance of changing and disrupting harmful thoughts and behaviors that have solidified into repeating patterns. Mammals are habitual creatures with brains that create well-worn paths of routines. Humans are no different. When we are children, our psyches are like diffuse, glowing lights shining in all directions. As adults, our minds are like a focused flashlight beam that always points in the same direction. This focus is due to the natural neuronal pruning of the brain as we mature.

Children are naturally open, curious, and keen to learn anything new. We are creative when we are young because our brains are still "plastic and fluid," meaning they grow and make new neuronal connections to prepare us to be adults that can survive without our mothers. By adulthood, most of us settle into a set of well-worn thought loops that help us conserve effort through waking life. We get out of bed and do the same morning routine; we drive to work the same way; we move through the office, eat the same lunch, and watch the same kinds of TV series—day after day, week after week, year after year.

Habit-bound thinking and behaviors give us the evolutionary advantage of figuring out the most efficient patterns to help us survive, allowing our organisms to idle with the least effort. We are hardwired to conserve energy. Experts in physical and mental health, such as Harvard researcher Dr. David Sinclair, have extensively researched the relationship between stress and aging. Sinclair's research focuses on "stress bodies," the cellular changes that occur in response to stress, and how these changes can impact health and longevity.

According to Sinclair, "stress bodies" are a natural stress response and are beneficial in small doses (Amorim et al. 2022). They help the human body adapt to changing conditions and increase disease resistance. However, chronic stress can lead to the accumulation of stress bodies, which can adversely affect health and aging. Sinclair's research has shown that the accumulation of stress bodies can contribute to the development of age-related diseases such as Alzheimer's, cancer, and heart disease. In contrast to chronic stress, the phenomenon of hormesis is a rebound effect that can have tonifying and recalibrating results after brief stresses. Examples include brief saunas, ice baths, fasting, and high-impact interval training. Although the acute stimulus is temporarily stressful, health benefits persist after homeostasis returns.

> Hormesis is defined as a dose-response phenomenon characterized by low-dose stimulation and high-dose inhibition and has been recognized as representing an overcompensation for mild environmental stress. The beneficial effects of mild stress on aging and longevity have been studied for many years. In experimental animals, mild dietary stress (dietary restriction, DR) without malnutrition delays most age-related physiological changes and extends maximum and average lifespan. Animal studies have also demonstrated that DR can prevent or lessen the severity of cancer, stroke, coronary heart disease, autoimmune disease, allergy,

Parkinson's disease, and Alzheimer's disease. The effects of DR are considered to result from hormetic mechanisms. These effects were reported by means of various DR regimens, such as caloric restriction, total-nutrient restriction, alternate-day fasting, and short-term fasting. Mild dietary stress, including restriction of amount or frequency of intake, is the essence of DR (Kouda and Iki 2010).

From an evolutionary point of view, it is reasonable to surmise that in moderate doses, this health-stimulating effect reminds our animal bodies that we are still alive and relevant; it keeps the fires burning and the lights on. A little stress leads to healthy adaptations and wellness, but too much stress leads to disease.

Human brains may have a similar, hormetic dynamic response to the body. The untasked or "idling" mind is called the default mode network (DMN). Like the body, the diminished range of thinking patterns characteristic of the DMN can be expanded through hormetic challenges, resulting in a renewed sense of possibility, openness, and creative agency. It is a network of regions and pathways involving different areas of the brain that run loops of habitual thinking patterns when not focusing on a task. Brain structures considered part of the DMN are the medial prefrontal cortex, posterior cingulate cortex, inferior parietal lobe, middle temporal lobe, and precuneus (Greicius et al. 2004).

One of the most extraordinary scientific findings about psychedelics is that they reduce the activity in the DMN. A functional magnetic resonance imaging (fMRI) scan is a neuroimaging technique that measures brain activity by detecting changes in blood flow. On fMRI scans, the DMN reveals lower levels of activity when the test subject is engaged in a particular task, such as paying attention, but higher levels of activity when subjects are awake and not involved in any specific mental exercise. Higher activation occurs when daydreaming, recalling memories, envisioning the future, monitoring the environment, thinking about the intentions of others, and engaging in whatever other mental activities occur when our minds are idling. This behavior also saves energy, making our "lights" less diffuse and more focused. This patterned way of thinking can also be limiting. At best, our loops are boring. At worst, our minds get stuck in trauma pattern thinking and a diminished range of possibilities.

Psychedelics allow and encourage the brain to make new neuronal connections, resulting in creative thinking and the breaking of old, looping thought patterns. These effects don't only last during the active psychedelic trip but days, weeks, and sometimes even months afterward. Psychedelics can rewire the brain to be less addicted, depressed, anxious, and traumatized. A study by Griffiths et al. (2016) found that a single dose of psilocybin resulted in decreased symptoms of depression and anxiety in patients with a life-threatening cancer diagnosis. Another study published in the journal *Psychopharmacology* in 2019 found that two doses of LSD significantly reduced anxiety symptoms in patients with life-threatening illnesses (Fuentes 2019), and Barrett et al. (2020) found that psilocybin therapy reduced symptoms of anhedonia (the inability to feel pleasure) and decreased neuroticism in patients with major depressive disorder.

Perhaps taking psychedelics is akin to hormesis for the brain by introducing new connectivity and suppressing habitual thinking patterns.

Psychedelic Medicine Is Hormesis for the Psyche

> *"The intense experience of a negative emotion,*
> *when allowed to run its course without interference,*
> *is the funeral pyre of that emotion."*
>
> —STANISLAV GROF, M.D., PH.D.

As discussed in the previous section, psychedelic experiences create a temporary challenge and therefore a kind of hormesis for the psyche. If it is stressful, one might wonder why to subject oneself to the possibility of a "bad trip." Psychedelic medicine facilitates healing when experienced within a proper healing container, with adequate preparation, support, and full integration. However, the length of time and number of sessions required varies from person to person. The process is nonlinear and impossible to predict. Many "bad trips" are repressed traumatic memories revealing themselves. The psyche isn't prepared to digest them, or the journeyer may not be in a safe container to work through the material. Perhaps the journey may reveal a truth the psyche is not yet ready to see, which underscores the importance of a well-trained, ethical, and adept facilitator to assist the process.

I don't believe there are any "bad trips;" I trust that these medicines can produce more of our latent intelligence to bring us home to our true Selves. Confronting fears, guilt, and ugly dynamics offers us opportunities to learn and grow, but this requires a larger view. People aren't healed in one therapy session or a single psychedelic journey. Working with psychedelic medicines is a relational process, not a one-time visit. From the more expansive vantage point of several journeys, we can usually see a logic in the grand trajectory. A so-called bad trip is often followed by a blissful journey. Patience and tenacity are required for seekers who want to receive complete healing from these medicines.

A Difficult Journey Is Not a Bad Trip

> *"The very cave you are afraid to enter turns out to be the source of what you are looking for.*
> *The damned thing in the cave that was so dreaded has become the center."*

—JOSEPH CAMPBELL

After decades of psychedelic prohibition propaganda, concerns about "bad trips" linger in the popular imagination. I would be remiss if I didn't discuss challenging psychedelic journeys. Recently there has been a

180-degree shift in popular media, reflecting their eagerness to seize upon the promise of psychedelic medicine's potential to heal all our emotional woes. This has downplayed how common it is to suffer a challenging or even agonizing psychedelic experience.

Many journeyers are shocked when, despite their level of self-development and practice, they are still overwhelmed by powerful or disquieting experiences that humble them.

Difficult journeys are much more common for those who have not adequately prepared, don't have a safe and well-planned set and setting, or are using/ingesting substances that interfere with the medicines, for example, not adhering to the proper ayahuasca diet. Difficult content can arise from unresolved traumatic experiences. Journeyers may receive direction to take accountability for past harmful behaviors and attitudes towards others and oneself during a psychedelic journey and make amends where needed. There may be a recognition of destructive lifestyles or emotional patterns, fears, phobias, control routines, etc. A skilled IFS therapist can help the journeyer understand these as burdened parts.

Even the most skilled and experienced psychonauts have challenging journeys from time to time. Hard trips are expected and understood as part of the healing process. In Jungian terms, shadow worlds balance the light and love realms. We live in a society that wants life to be a safe and secure Disneyland ride with guard rails and seatbelts. Modern people possessed by the juvenile puer archetype stay in prisons of positivity and spiritual bypassing. Before medicine journeys, it is essential to educate clients that difficult experiences are part of the process, and there is unpredictability with these substances, no matter how well we prepare.

The good news is even the most challenging experiences may be given meaning and woven into the tapestry of the Heroine's/Hero's Journey.

When developing his theory of the Hero's Journey, Joseph Campbell was inspired by Nietzsche:

Nietzsche was the one who did the job for me. At a certain moment in his life, the idea came to him of what he called "the love of your fate." Whatever your fate is, whatever the hell happens, you say, "This is what I need." It may look like a wreck, but go at it as though it were an opportunity, a challenge. If you bring love to that moment—not discouragement—you will find the strength is there. Any disaster you can survive is an improvement in your character, your stature, and your life. What a privilege! This is when the spontaneity of your own nature will have a chance to flow.

Then, when looking back at your life, you will see that the moments which seemed to be great failures followed by wreckage were the incidents that shaped the life you have now. You'll see that this is really true. Nothing can happen to you that is not positive. Even though it looks and feels at the moment like a negative crisis, it is not. The crisis throws you back, and when you are required to exhibit strength it comes. (Campbell 1991).

The presuppositions of the Theradelic Approach assert that humans are innately good and moral, and the human psyche will move toward healing naturally when the blocks to well-being are removed. It also asserts that psychedelic experiences contain inherent wisdom, and in the larger trajectory of working with them, even bad trips, given context in a larger framework of healing, are intrinsic and essential to the work.

5

INFLUENCES

Internal Family Systems and the Hero's/Heroine's Journey

A powerful component of the Theradelic Approach is to explain the symbolic content experienced in dreams, hypnosis, and psychedelic journeys as communications from the depths of the internal ecosystem. One could say that archetypes are parts conveying themselves symbolically. I have found that organizing therapy treatment around the Hero's/Heroine's Journey can help create resilience, nurture a positive explanatory style, and internalize the locus of control. Because archetypes are already woven into our psyches through dreams, fantasies, and storytelling, this method is highly intuitive and quickly adopted by clients. To simplify it, we can use archetypes and the Hero's/Heroine's Journey from within the IFS framework. A core concept is developing the ability to use symbols and metaphors within psychedelic journeys, dreams, daydreams, or meditations to be processed and integrated using the IFS healing-steps framework. The process of using archetypes within the IFS framework is a delightfully creative and effective way to work with psychedelics. Let me offer you an example. I have changed identifying information in the case stories shared in this book to protect patient identities.

One of my therapy clients had a series of ketamine journeys that involved powerful imagery around trees. On one trip, she was a little girl and approached an enormous pine tree. Her childlike energy body sat and meditated, leaning against the strong trunk. The tree made her feel very safe. Whenever she got lost in the psychedelic space, she would return to this tree and sit underneath it. There were many symbolic images involving the pine tree. She saw that she was a pine cone. She experienced herself as a sapling. As we explored the meaning of how the symbol of the tree was *for her* and what part it might be in her psyche, we realized it was a strong protector that was a Self-like part. Its roots symbolized staying grounded and strong, and its branches represented reaching into the sky and trying new things. The pine cone was her nascent Self-like part that was gaining clarity and confidence. She realized its reference to the pineal gland and awakening. This Self-like part of her was a powerful protector that guided her whenever she felt lost. These symbols became totems for her to return to whenever she wanted to reconnect with this Self-like protector who always offered guidance. Her Self-led parts showed her the pine tree imagery to connect the exiles and managers to Self-leadership.

Archetypal Psychology

Jungians understand that there is a mythic imaginal realm where archetypes and the collective unconscious transcend individual experience. Both IFS and archetypal psychology use symbolism, but archetypal psychology deals with universal imagery the subconscious interprets. IFS works locally within the individual's parts and allows the client and all of their parts to direct the meaning. In other words, archetypal psychology and IFS are compatible conceptual frameworks but differ in scope. IFS is practical and applied integration, whereas archetypal psychology tries to accomplish the same goal but usually uses indirect means. Though archetypal and Jungian psychology differ in the ontological placement of archetypes, both methodologies place the imaginal realm as the primary place where experience is generated and processed. Of the archetypal approach, psychologist James Hillman said:

Rather, following Jung, I use the word fantasy-image in the poetic sense, considering images to be the basic givens of psychic life, self-originating, inventive, spontaneous, complete, and organized in archetypal patterns. Fantasy images are raw materials and finished products of the psyche, and they are the privileged mode of access to knowledge of the soul. Nothing is more primary. Every notion in our minds, each perception of the world, and sensation in ourselves must go through a psychic organization to "happen." Every single feeling or observation occurs as a psychic event by forming a fantasy image (Hillman 1989, 22).

Both Jung and Hillman agree on the psychic "facts" of archetypes as mediums of meaning. Jung asserts that images and archetypes emerge as forms of the human collective unconscious, serving as a cross-cultural index of imaginative activity. However, Hillman asserts that the imaginal realm is primary and exists as the medium intrinsic to consciousness. Jung is looking at the collective shared experience, and Hillman focuses on the imaginal realm as the medium of perception itself. That relates to IFS because, whether you are in Self or burdened parts, from both vantage points, symbolic content can be viewed as archetypes.

Here is an example of using IFS and archetypal psychology with psychedelic medicine. A client may have an exiled part that is so utterly alienated, unwelcome, and protected by the system that it cannot be approached with direct verbal exchange. Direct contact is too overwhelming to the fragile exile and its protectors. However, during a psychedelic journey, guides or the Self might utilize archetypes and symbolism in the form of a beautiful poem, a nostalgic song, or a compelling visual image to send a message of hope to the vulnerable part. The intention is to bridge the gap and get a message through fear and mistrust. Later, a direct verbal exchange may be more possible when trust is built. Read more about this process in Chapter Ten.

The Heroine's and Hero's Journey: Making Meaning

"Jung represents human consciousness,
something like a field, a magnetic field.
As soon as the Content falls into the field of consciousness,
it falls into a web of associations."

—MARIE-LOUISE VON FRANZ, *CREATION MYTHS*

An essential component of the Theradelic Approach is the view of our life patterns as macro and micro trajectories that travel along the Heroine's/ Hero's Journey. Telling one's life myth with a positive explanatory style creates meaning from life's trials. Internalizing the locus of control creates proactive responses to external events (rather than reacting). Mapping life challenges through the lens of the Hero's/Heroine's Journey is constructive. Situating visionary contents in a mythic progression helps convert bewildering and sometimes overwhelming experiences into a meaningful story arc. The Hero's/Heroine's Journey is a healing narrative for clients and a way to internalize a new locus of control in themselves, one with an optimistic cast. This matters to the Theradelic Approach because meaningless suffering is agony, but harnessing the power of suffering in transformation empowers a better narrative to emerge and enhances a sense of agency.

The comparative mythologist Dr. Joseph Campbell expanded the concept of the Hero's Journey in 1949. In his famous book *The Hero with a Thousand Faces*, he describes the narrative pattern:

> A hero ventures forth from the world of common day into
> a region of supernatural wonder: fabulous forces are there
> encountered, and a decisive victory is won: the hero comes back
> from this mysterious adventure with the power to bestow boons on
> his fellow man (Campbell 1949).

It's worth mentioning the Hero's Journey popularized by Campbell builds on previous work by Marie-Louise von Franz, a Swiss Jungian analyst and scholar who wrote about the Hero's Journey and its connection to Jungian psychology. She was a close colleague and collaborator of Carl Jung and was instrumental in developing and expanding upon his ideas. In her book *The Feminine in Fairy Tales,* von Franz explores the archetype of the hero and the Hero's Journey as it appears in fairy tales and myths. She notes that the Hero's Journey represents the process of individuation or the journey toward becoming a whole and integrated person.

Von Franz also examines the role of the feminine in the Hero's Journey, noting that the hero often encounters a wise woman or goddess figure who serves as a guide or mentor. She suggests that this figure represents the feminine aspect of the psyche, which is often undervalued in patriarchal societies but is essential to individuation.

Later, after both von Franz and Campbell, a version for women, the Heroine's Journey, was developed by Maureen Murdock in 1990 when she published *The Heroine's Journey: Woman's Quest for Wholeness* in response to Campbell's Hero's Journey model. Murdock was a Jungian psychotherapist and a student of Joseph Campbell. She stated that the Heroine's Journey is healing the wounding that exists deep within each woman and the larger culture.

In my view, the Hero's/Heroine's Journey doesn't necessarily need to be gendered, and the twelve stages outlined below apply in archetypal patterns for women, men, or any gender identity. The Heroine/Hero's Journey has twelve stages. I will use the terms "hero" and "heroine" interchangeably.

The 12 Stages of the Heroine's/Hero's Journey

The reason the twelve stages of the Heroine's/Hero's Journey are important to the Theradelic Approach is that these steps of the narrative arc frequently form the architecture of human storytelling, whether it is a movie, fairy tale, psychedelic vision, or personal adventure. The storytelling Self organizes in psychedelic visions, and therapists can harness this organizing principle by weaving a narrative with a redemptive moral dimension to enhance the sense of discovery, challenge, and purpose.

1. **The Ordinary World.** Where we meet and identify with the hero. The hero is known and seemingly ordinary.

2. **The Call to Adventure.** A challenge or quest is proposed. Likely, an event, conflict, or problem prompts the adventure.

3. **Refusal of the Call.** The heroine initially rejects this call because of fear, hesitation, insecurity, or another reason. Whatever the reason, the call to adventure is initially denied.

4. **Meeting the Mentor.** The mentor helps the hero gain confidence and gives insight or advice to overcome fears.

5. **Crossing the Threshold.** This signifies that the heroine has committed to the journey.

6. **Tests, Allies, Enemies.** The hero needs to learn who can be trusted. A sidekick emerges.

7. **Approach to the Innermost Cave.** Preparations are needed and might include maps and reconnaissance to enter the cave.

8. **The Ordeal.** This is the greatest fear and most difficult challenge. The work is challenging but worth the reward.

CHAPTER FIVE | INFLUENCES

9. **Reward (Seizing the Sword).** What is most feared is faced with courage.

10. **The Road Back.** The heroine recommits to completing the journey and accepts the road back to the ordinary world.

11. **The Resurrection.** This can be the hero's most dangerous life-and-death ordeal and is the story's climax. There is a final test that represents a cleansing. It might be a showdown between the heroine and the shadow. During the resurrection, one final challenge awaits.

12. **Return with the Elixir.** The final reward after the hero is resurrected, purified, and returns to the ordinary world.

As clients are recounting their psychedelic experiences, the therapist can use the twelve steps of the Hero's/Heroine's Journey as a loose framework to orient and face the challenges, triumphs, and resolution of the trip and its integration. It usually takes several therapy sessions, complete with several journeys and integration, to frame the trajectory into the heroine's/hero's narrative.

The Intrinsic Drive Toward Creating Meaning and Stories

*"There is not one big cosmic meaning for all;
there is only the meaning we each give to our life, an individual meaning,
an individual plot, like an individual novel, a book for each person."*

—ANAÏS NIN

Von Franz's, Campbell's, and Murdock's contributions were to show us the fundamental structure of storytelling. They showed us humans have a proclivity for myth.

89

Weaving a story to create meaning is human beings' most innate natural process. I would offer that the main evolutionary driver of Homo sapiens is the capacity of storytelling as a way to understand our world. When we were nomadic and couldn't carry much, if anything, we always had our stories. They are our most intimate resource, and we carry them with us everywhere. Humans have only recently owned property: land, houses, livestock, books, cars, etc. Property ownership has informed our self-identities, and we have come to develop religions that tell us we are defined in a particular way: concrete, with static bodies, minds, and souls, with individual identities and specific locations in time-space reality. It is interesting to imagine what our identities might have been like before we owned physical resources. Perhaps we didn't see ourselves as separate but as part of a tribe and nature. For most of human prehistory, we were nomadic hunters and gatherers. Most of human history occurred before written language. Hunter-gatherer cultures relied on oral history to carry knowledge.

Stories were told socially, not as idle pastimes but as essential knowledge transmissions for group survival. Shared stories concerned what was safe to eat, where the hunting was good, where to find reliable sources of water, and where there was space away from danger to build temporary shelters. These stories were shared through families and tribes and passed down through generations. Stories were foundational to enabling humans to survive and become the dominant species on Earth. Stories allowed humans to organize in large groups and build upon prior knowledge from previous generations and other cultures, creating more social complexity.

Oral knowledge doesn't weigh down nomadic people. It is carried in the psyche and shared by voice through stories and songs. Over time, the stories became more complex, and woven into them were myths explaining why nature works the way it does. Mythic lore explained why people died and where they went, the seasons' cycles, the stars' trajectory, and the mysteries of the universe. Our large brains evolved to hold countless complex stories about survival, numinosity, spirituality, and myths.

Creating a personal mythology based on our lives' challenges and triumphs is a creative process that makes use of narrative powers to enhance healing through a sense of agency. I once had a severely depressed client who was a self-proclaimed nihilist and skeptic. He was brilliantly intelligent, and we had many interesting discussions about whether life had meaning or the universe was mere chaos. My style of therapy was definitely at odds with his view of reality—that life was futile, chaotic, and meaningless. I suspected he sought me out and remained a client because I challenged his nihilist part. I was an external embodiment of a polarized, hopeful part within his psyche that he wanted to internalize. But first, we had to satisfy his skeptical, intellectual parts by debating. In addition, this process distracted us from getting deeper into accessing his exiles if we spent the therapy hour arguing about the meaning of life.

Finally, one day I said something like, "Humans have evolved to be incredible storytellers because we need stories to weave us together in prosocial communities. Storytelling is the greatest strength of humankind—that we can create collective mythologies and cooperate to do highly complex things. We're like honeybees mixed with chimpanzees! We've been telling myths and stories since we lived in caves. Every culture, throughout time, has had a mythology that gives life meaning and structure. Nihilism is no different—it's a mythology, too, one that has an external locus of control, a negative explanatory style, and encourages learned helplessness. Out of all the amazing mythologies to adopt as your own, while knowing you require meaning because you are a member of Homo sapiens, why would you choose one that makes you feel terrible? If you are truly a skeptic, you need to be a skeptic of nihilism too." Becoming skeptical of his skepticism, and realizing he was still weaving mythology for himself, one of nihilism, seemed to shift him momentarily. Shortly after this conversation, he had a breakthrough that took the course of his life in a completely new direction.

Embracing the Ineffable and the Numinous

*"We are on the lookout for a fuller expression and
a wider frame within which to view things.
Allow the extravagant tenderness of God to wash over us.
Permit the lavishing of such love to surround and fill us,
then go into the world and speak the whole language.
This is the fluency of the mystic.
Who chooses to live in the soul, inhabiting the tender fragrance of love?
The longing of the mystic is to be at home with yourself and then
put out the welcome mat so that others find a home within you.
In this, we want to be all there."*

—FATHER GREGORY BOYLE

However we define God—the Universe, the Goddess, the Divine—Father Boyle captures the energy of it eloquently. Putting out the welcome mat so others can find a home in us is the path of the compassionate soul. I am grateful for the many teachers, mentors, and guides in the living and spirit world who guide me and for psychedelic experiences that have woven meaning into my life myth.

Mystical and numinous experiences are often described as profound encounters with a divine or transcendent reality that is beyond the ordinary, everyday worlds. These experiences are characterized by a sense of unity and interconnectedness with all things, a feeling of ineffable awe and wonder, and a profound sense of peace, love, and understanding. Mystical experiences are often described as a direct encounter with the divine, while numinous experiences are a sense of awe and reverence for the mysterious and unknown.

Psychedelic journeys have been known to facilitate these types of experiences, often providing a catalyst for profound shifts in consciousness. An often-overlooked component of the psychedelic experience is described as the numinous, but the numinous isn't only the ineffable. It comes from the root Latin word *numen*, which refers to a divine or supernatural power or presence. In psychedelic experiences, a sense of cherishing and compelling importance often results in transformative experiences. Ultimately, the mystical and numinous experiences that can be facilitated by psychedelic journeys offer a glimpse into a world that is beyond the rational mind and the limitations of our everyday experience and can help us to connect with a more profound sense of purpose and meaning in our lives.

Psychedelics may bring us back to a place where we are a connected hive mind rather than individual, separate consciousnesses. Mental illness has occurred throughout history, and the way we perceive mental health is relative to cultural norms. When humans lived in communities, the support of the tribe ameliorated mental illness. Modern life exacerbates mental disease due to social isolation, socioeconomic strife, and stress. The pressures of modern society seem to stimulate anxiety, depression, and trauma. There's so much pressure to perform at all times that people outside the automaton paradigm have difficulty navigating the system that requires so much complex, sequential thinking.

Connection and belonging mitigate the sense of isolation and separateness. Sometimes I've wondered if our yearning for God and heaven is an innate afterimage of how we evolved to connect to our animal, plant, and fungi kin. We desire to go home and merge again into the One.

When I emerged from a psychedelic experience once, I exclaimed, "I used to be afraid there is nothing after we die. Now I am afraid it is EVERYTHING after we die!" There was an immersive sense of being connected to everything rather than separate and alone. The experience felt overwhelming, and the vastness of "everything" was excruciatingly blissful.

Psychedelic medicine draws us into mystical experiences. The journeys are ineffable; human language cannot capture the full spectrum of meaning and emotion they give us. We as practitioners must not dismiss the meaningfulness and spiritual impact that psychedelic journeys bring many people. Staying curious and using the client's specific mystical language helps support the numinous experiences.

Prominent Influences in Trauma and Psychedelic Therapy

The Theradelic Approach has been influenced by many great mentors I have had the honor of working with throughout my career. Through working with psychedelics, I have also been greatly influenced by the natural world.

Richard Schwartz: IFS

Internal Family Systems (IFS) is a therapeutic model developed by Richard Schwartz in the 1980s. The model is based on the idea that the mind consists of different parts or "subpersonalities" that can have conflicting interests and emotions. IFS therapy is a process of identifying and working with these parts to help people understand their inner workings and promote healing and self-regulation.

Richard Schwartz initially trained as a family therapist and developed the IFS model to understand and work with the inner conflicts he observed in his clients. One of the key concepts of IFS is the idea of the "Self," which is the part of the mind that is calm, centered, and connected to the individual's values and sense of purpose. According to IFS, the Self is capable of leading the therapy process, and by accessing it, people can gain clarity and insight into their inner workings. The Self has eight intrinsic qualities: curiosity, compassion, clarity, connectedness, creativity, courage, confidence, and calm.

IFS therapy is effective for many issues, including trauma, anxiety, depression, and addiction. Research has also shown that it can benefit people with eating disorders, chronic pain, personality disorders, and many other issues. A study by Baldwin et al. (2011) found that IFS therapy was effective in reducing symptoms of PTSD in veterans, and another study by Anderson and colleagues (2019) found it was effective in reducing symptoms of depression in people with a history of childhood abuse.

IFS therapy is based on the idea that each subpersonality or "part" has a positive intent. By understanding and working with these parts, individuals can access their inner wisdom and resources to promote healing and growth. In IFS, the therapist acts as a guide, helping people to turn inwards for "in-sight," to identify, understand, and work with their different parts, and to develop a relationship with their Selves. Optimally, the client talks to their different parts with the therapist's guidance. This results in Self-leadership of the parts.

Since the development of the model, IFS has gained popularity and been integrated into many different therapeutic approaches, such as cognitive behavioral therapy (CBT), psychoanalytic therapy, and somatic experiencing.

IFS dovetails beautifully with psychedelic-assisted psychotherapy and is the therapeutic modality I use most often. Dr. Schwartz understands psychedelic medicines as a way to access Self energy and rapidly unburden parts. As discussed in greater detail in Section Three of this book, there are specific ways to utilize IFS with psychedelics to create safety and potentiate healing. We have worked together, creating several trainings and retreats merging IFS with psychedelic-assisted psychotherapy.

Bessel van der Kolk, Gabor Maté: Psychedelics, Addiction, and Trauma

Two prominent figures in the trauma research field are Dr. Bessel van der Kolk and Dr. Gabor Maté. Both have significantly contributed to our understanding of trauma and its effects on the mind and body.

Bessel van der Kolk is a psychiatrist and researcher who has been studying trauma's effects for over four decades. He has conducted extensive research on the impact of childhood abuse and neglect. He has developed a theoretical model that highlights the role of the body in the experience and aftermath of trauma. Van der Kolk's work emphasizes the importance of addressing the biological and physiological effects of trauma and its psychological impact. Van der Kolk's technique is called "trauma-centered psychotherapy" and emphasizes the role of the body in the healing process. Dr. van der Kolk has become an enthusiastic supporter of psychedelic-assisted psychotherapy to facilitate the processes of trauma healing. He stresses the importance of proceeding carefully with powerful psychedelic experiences, as they can open up vulnerabilities within people with trauma histories.

Dr. Gabor Maté is a physician and researcher who has focused on the impact of trauma on individuals and communities. He has researched the effects of childhood trauma, including neglect and abuse, on the development of addiction and mental health disorders. Dr. Maté's work emphasizes the importance of addressing the social and environmental factors contributing to trauma and its effects. Dr. Maté has developed a "trauma-informed care approach," emphasizing the importance of addressing social and environmental factors in the healing process. He has explored the potential of ayahuasca in treating addiction. Dr. Mate's research suggests that ayahuasca can help individuals struggling with addiction by addressing the underlying emotional and psychological causes of their addictive behaviors. His work with ayahuasca and addiction involves a combination of traditional Amazonian shamanic practices and Western psychotherapeutic techniques. Through this process, patients can better understand their addictive behaviors and work towards healing and transformation. His research has shown promising results, with individuals reporting significant improvements in their addictive behaviors and reductions in anxiety, depression, and other mental health issues.

Both researchers have contributed to recognizing trauma's complexity and multidimensional nature, emphasizing that it is not only a psychological issue but also a physiological and social issue that requires a comprehensive approach. They have also highlighted the importance of addressing the effects of trauma in early life, as it can have long-term impacts on individuals and communities.

William and Brian Richards: Psilocybin Research

Two prominent figures in the psilocybin research field who have inspired me are father and son Dr. William (Bill) Richards and Dr. Brian Richards. Both have been involved in psilocybin research for several decades. The Richards have significantly contributed to understanding the compound's effects and therapeutic potential.

Bill Richards has researched the effects of psilocybin on perception, cognition, and emotion and the long-term effects of psilocybin use. He has emphasized the importance of understanding the subjective experiences of people who use psilocybin and has been a proponent of using the compound in therapeutic conditions. He has researched the use of psilocybin in religious and spiritual contexts and has also studied the therapeutic potential of psilocybin for people with a terminal illnesses.

Brian and Bill Richards have contributed to the renewed interest in psilocybin research, which has seen a resurgence in recent years. They have also emphasized the importance of providing a safe and supportive environment for people using psilocybin in therapeutic contexts. An excellent book on psychedelics is Bill Richards' *Sacred Knowledge*.

Stanislav Grof: LSD Research and Holotropic Breathwork

A prominent figure in early psychedelic research is psychiatrist Dr. Stanislav Grof, who was involved in pre-prohibition LSD research. Grof began researching the therapeutic potential of LSD in the 1950s and 1960s, and during this time, he administered LSD to thousands of patients in controlled therapeutic settings. He observed that the LSD experience could lead to profound emotional and psychological healing and that it could also facilitate spiritual and transpersonal experiences, often via a supported crisis.

Grof's clinical experience led him to develop the concept of "perinatal matrices," which refers to the idea that experiences of birth and death are stored in the unconscious mind and can be accessed through nonordinary states of consciousness. This concept has been influential in the field of transpersonal psychology and psychotherapy.

When LSD was made illegal in 1970, Grof and his wife, Christina, developed Holotropic Breathwork. This therapeutic approach incorporates nonordinary states of consciousness for healing and self-exploration. Holotropic Breathwork uses a specific pattern of breathing, music, and bodywork to access nonordinary states of consciousness. It has been used to address various psychological and physical issues. Dr. Grof proposed the concept of "birth trauma matrices," the idea that traumatic experiences before, during, and after birth can impact a person's psychological and spiritual development. These matrices can manifest as physical and emotional symptoms, influencing one's worldview and sense of self. Breath is used in Holotropic Breathwork to reach an altered state of consciousness where we can process the birth trauma matrices, among many other phenomena.

Francine Shapiro: EMDR

Eye movement desensitization and reprocessing (EMDR) is a psychotherapy approach Francine Shapiro developed in the late 1980s. EMDR is based on the idea that traumatic memories are stored in the brain in an unprocessed memory form. By bringing these memories to mind and using specific eye movements or other forms of bilateral stimulation, the memories can be processed and integrated into the individual's overall life experiences. This process leads to a reduction in symptoms of trauma.

EMDR therapy typically involves the therapist guiding the client to bring a traumatic memory to mind while engaging in eye movements or other forms of bilateral stimulation. The therapist will assist the client in identifying and processing any negative beliefs or emotions associated with the memory. The goal of EMDR is to help the client integrate the traumatic memory into regular memory storage, reducing trauma symptoms.

Research has shown that EMDR treats many conditions, including PTSD, anxiety, and depression. A meta-analysis of research studies by van Etten and Taylor (1998) found that EMDR was as effective as other types of psychotherapy in treating PTSD and may be more effective than other treatments in some cases. A study by Rothbaum et al. (2005) found that EMDR was effective in reducing symptoms of PTSD in people with a history of childhood abuse.

Various professional organizations have recognized EMDR therapy as an evidence-based treatment for PTSD. In 2017, the World Health Organization (WHO) included EMDR in its list of recommended treatments for PTSD (Castelnuovo, Fernandez, and Amann 2019). The American Psychiatric Association, the International Society for Traumatic Stress Studies, and the Department of Veterans Affairs also support the use of EMDR.

The approach has been widely adopted, and many trained practitioners in different countries use it in their practices. EMDR therapy can be completed relatively quickly. It has also been used to treat other conditions such as phobias, panic disorder, and acute stress disorder.

John Gottman: Couples Therapy and Attachment Theory

John Gottman is a renowned psychologist and researcher known for his work on couples and relationships. He co-founded The Gottman Institute, which is dedicated to researching and promoting healthy relationships. One of his most notable contributions is the development of the Gottman

Method for couples therapy, based on his study of couples' communication dynamics and feedback loops.

The Gottman Method is a research-based, cognitive behavioral approach to couples therapy that focuses on improving communication, increasing intimacy, and resolving conflicts. It is grounded in attachment theory, which posits that human beings have a fundamental need for secure attachments to others and that relationship satisfaction and stability are closely tied to the quality of these attachments. The Gottman Method helps couples identify and address the underlying issues causing problems in their relationship. It teaches them the skills to build a stronger and more satisfying bond by creating emotional kindness, generosity, and safety within the couple or family system.

Gottman and his team extensively researched couples using observational, self-reporting, and physiological measures. Their studies have shown that the Gottman Method effectively improves relationship satisfaction, reduces conflict, and increases intimacy. A meta-analysis of studies by Davoodvandi, Navabi Nejad, and Farzad (2018) found that couples therapy based on the Gottman Method effectively improves relationship satisfaction and reduces distress.

Nature as an Influence on Psychedelic Therapy

Psychedelics frequently produce mystical experiences; some people perceive these as a way to communicate with the natural world or even with some spiritual realms. Nature is often closely associated with psychedelic experiences. Nature is my church, and I feel the most connected to spirituality and the sacred when I spend time outdoors. The beauty of the natural world can be a powerful source of inspiration and insight during a psychedelic journey. Many plant-based psychedelic substances are derived from natural sources, and consuming them in nature can further enhance the sense of connection to the natural world. The natural setting provides a sense of safety and tranquility that helps to facilitate a deeper and more meaningful psychedelic experience.

Many people report that the natural world appears more vibrant and alive during a psychedelic experience, with colors and patterns becoming more intense and seemingly vibrating with vitality and aliveness. The heightened perception of the natural world can lead to a greater appreciation of its beauty and complexity and inspire a profound sense of awe and wonder. Psychedelics can help to re-establish a connection to the natural world, often lost in modern society.

Psychedelics frequently produce mystical experiences; some people perceive these as a way to communicate with the natural world or even with some spiritual realms. This epoch beckons us to return to our innate desire for a close relationship with the natural world. We must heed this call before we destroy its diversity and wonder. I feel passionate about offering these medicines to help us return "home" to the earth and reconnect with our plant, animal, fungi, and mineral brothers and sisters.

6
THE THERAPIST

*"If there is anything that we wish to change in the child,
we should first examine it
and see whether it is not something
that could better be changed in ourselves."*

—C.G. JUNG, *THE INTEGRATION OF THE PERSONALITY*

This chapter covers practices and pitfalls of being an effective and ethical psychedelic practitioner. There are many aspects to cover, from doing your own work in therapy, the importance of training, collaborating, and receiving mentoring from other professionals to ethics, building attachment, and creating rapport with clients. Psychedelics are powerful tools, and with greater power comes greater responsibility. I cannot overstate how profoundly different psychedelic-assisted psychotherapy is from any other therapeutic modality. There is simply no way for the therapist to be separate from the journeyer's experience during a psychedelic trip. The profound enhancement of mental energy from the therapist's presence produces intense suggestibility and sensitivity for the journeyer. Our way of being with others is felt and understood on a psychic level. Our comfort with our internal psychic ecosystem, client relationship and rapport, and trust and knowledge of the medicine is sensed in the heightened awareness activated by psychedelics. Who we are in our *being* in the world is essential. What we do in our daily patterns shines through. Living from a place of integrity, honesty, and ethics inside and outside the therapy office is pertinent to how we hold space for our clients. Expect the client to see past our compartmentalizations.

Journeyers are incredibly vulnerable, suggestible, and sensitive when engaging with the psychedelic realms. The safety and well-being of our clients are paramount. We do not need to be perfect, but we need to be acutely self-aware and able to track our activated parts, projections, and countertransference in real time.

Do Your Work in Therapy

> *"Knowing your own darkness is the best method*
> *for dealing with the darknesses of other people."*
>
> —C.G. JUNG, IN A LETTER TO KENDIG B. CULLY

Many of us entered the psychology field because we are wounded, which gives us great sensitivity and insight into the suffering of others. An interest in mental health and the vision of helping others is often a sublimated desire to help ourselves and our loved ones. Some of us began developing the role of pseudo-therapists to our families of origin when we were parentified, caretaking children. These parentified parts can become internalized as young protectors of even younger exiles. It isn't a problem if this was how we propelled ourselves into the helping fields, but it is a problem if we stay ignorant of our psychological systems and project our unmet needs and wounding onto our patients.

We become aware of this only by working with a skillful therapist ourselves. I am continually amazed at how common it is for mental healthcare workers not to meet regularly with a personal psychotherapist. Many mental health practitioners have never received psychotherapy. It's like being a chef who has never tasted their own cooking or a fitness trainer who doesn't or hasn't ever exercised. A psychologist once said in response to my skeptical reaction after he announced he'd never gone to a psychologist himself, "Why would I need it? Does a physician have to try every pharmaceutical medicine before prescribing it?" This assertion is a false equivalency based on pathologizing the need for psychotherapy. It assumes that the mental health clinician is above and beyond having any psychological challenges themselves. We live in a challenging time, and every single person has some level of psychological wounding. Beyond that, everyone would benefit from becoming more self-aware. Everyone would benefit from quality psychotherapy.

Sometimes therapists may project damaged exiles onto clients. This could stem from a misguided effort to feign perfection and disown burdened parts. We may defend against our vulnerabilities and become blended with perfectionist parts who desire insulation from revealing the reality that we are wounded ourselves. We want to profess to be experts on other peoples' psychology, and somehow that gets conflated with the need to be void of damage in ourselves. To use IFS language, we get so good at holding space for our therapy patients that we often develop protectors and managers that are very convincing "Self-like parts." They are so compelling that sometimes they seduce even us into believing we are perfectly healed and secure. These manager parts are essential in participating in a helping profession. However, are we aware that we have these parts and that they may be protecting vulnerable exiled parts?

Do your work. Explore your mind, your history, and your parts. Polish the multifaceted diamond within you so that you may reflect the divine more clearly.

Know Thyself

"To know thyself is the beginning of wisdom."

—SOCRATES

Do your psychedelic work too. There is no better way to become an incredible psychedelic facilitator than to become intimate with the psychedelic medicine you are facilitating. One experience isn't enough. I advise at least ten experiential journeys before offering psychedelic medicine to clients. Psychedelics open us to other planes of reality, each with different physics, signatures, and inhabitants. They also open us to dimensions within ourselves that we may not have accessed before. Developing a relationship with each medicine is beneficial in becoming a great facilitator and a more self-aware person. Understand the landscape and where the psyche may go during psychedelic journeys. Directly experience the afterglow and aftereffects of the medicine. Experience the importance of set and setting, preparation, how the space is held, and the integration process for yourself.

Work with different therapists who hold space for psychedelic journeys and sense how their energy informs the experience. No substitute, book, training, lecture, or class can come close to replacing the direct psychedelic experience.

Mentors and Colleagues

Seek ways to be mentored by experienced practitioners in the psychedelic field. Find mentors who have an "energy signature" you admire. Look into their backgrounds and what their clients and communities say and feel about them. Notice how you feel in their presence. Track your internal ecosystem. Do your parts feel safe, seen, and relaxed with them? Do they have the time and interest to mentor you?

Create a network of colleagues with a similar level of experience with psychedelic medicines to yours. Engage in group case consultations and skill-building sessions and share resources, studies, articles, and information about best practices. Network at conferences and attend training sessions and classes.

I have had so many exciting experiences in this field. There is a "Wild West" energy to psychedelic medicine as many people rush in to put their stakes in the ground and push everyone else out. Sometimes people behave in possessive and competitive ways. I have also been delighted to find many generous and gracious professionals welcoming me and others into the space.

Many psychedelic therapists are interested in collaborating and helping one another navigate this blossoming field. "Aboveground" medicalized psychedelics versus "underground" plant-medicine practitioners are among the more prominent polarized viewpoints.

There are many valid orientations to offer and many different psychedelic medicines, each with its own signature. They are wonderfully varied and polyvalent. Humans, animals, and the climate are in serious trouble. Humans suffer a worldwide epidemic of depression, anxiety, and trauma because we live in a traumatizing, socially isolating culture. Psychedelic medicines and the process surrounding them can help alleviate suffering. The more practitioners we can adequately train and educate, the more help we can get into the world. There are many ways to provide these experiences ethically and within best-practice standards. However, within the breadth of possibilities on where, when, and how the specific medicine is served and facilitated, three hard and fast rules apply globally and are consistently valid:

1.   The safety and well-being of the journeyer are of utmost importance.

2.   The facilitator's ethics, skill, experience, and integrity are central to the experience.

3.   Consent, in its broadest meaning, is to be obtained at every step along the entire trajectory of the psychedelic experience.

These three rules are always essential, without exception.

Proper Training

I have trained diverse groups of psychotherapists, physicians, psychiatrists, and nurses in experiential psychedelic-assisted psychotherapy. In this practice, I have come to recognize most are burned out. Being a psychotherapist specializing in trauma is akin to being an emotional janitor who endlessly cleans up after a toxic culture. The exhausted and burned-out therapists and physicians at my trainings intuit that incorporating psychedelics into their clinical practices will make their jobs easier by doing the heavy lifting in the sessions. Inevitably, in experiential training sessions, our messy psychological processes come up.

When, at last, these healthcare workers not only understand their experiences but also have the training and skills to handle the gravity of darkness they've been carrying, there is often a blossoming of buried traumatized exiles that bubble to the surface. Therapists are often wounded themselves. We have come to this professional sector because we recognize the urgent need for healers. We also exist in a damaged and systemically abusive culture. Mental healthcare workers have the added challenge of being further traumatized by listening to and seeing trauma daily at work.

I share this to inform you that if you go into psychedelic-assisted therapy, you should be prepared for how much challenging, unconscious material will repeatedly come up. This material may be triggering not only for the client but for you too. We are not outside the therapy container, but rather deep inside it and sometimes underwater. If you get lost in your clients' underworlds, learn how to swim back up to get air. Metaphorically, keep one foot in the underworld with a lantern to light the way and the other foot firmly earthside. It doesn't take courage only from the journeyer; it takes courage from the practitioner to fully attune to the intensity and diversity of the psychedelic realms. IFS and archetypal psychology assert that what is inside us is also outside us, and vice versa. Bring curiosity and openness because there is also exquisite beauty. There is healing, blessings, hope, compassion, and, most of all, love. Love is our inherent right and truth. The bad news is the world is messed up. The good news is it's all built outside a core of benevolent goodness and love. We don't have to go anywhere "out there." Our journey is to uncover all that is blocking the light that shines "in here."

I know many practitioners who offer beautiful, caring, and powerful work. To be like them, it's imperative that you seek training and experience. If you are interested in facilitating psychedelic journeys, at the very least, please:

- Receive **at least** one hundred hours of individual psychotherapy (not psychedelic) from a reputable therapist.
- Experience **at least** ten journeys receiving the medicine you are providing your clients under the guidance of a qualified psychedelic facilitator or an indigenous facilitator with equivalent experience and credibility.
- Undergo proper training from a reputable training organization. This can be tricky because many entities are now offering psychedelic training. Research your trainers' qualifications.
- Receive proper and thorough training in trauma from a reputable training organization, as this aspect will come up for many of your clients. I believe a psychedelic practitioner must be a licensed mental healthcare worker with at least a master's degree and additional training in psychological trauma care or have a cofacilitator who is trained to treat trauma.

Regarding Schedule I psychedelics, reputable training groups like MAPS have an experiential component, but it's usually not ten journeys. Completion of the MAPS training involves a single MDMA experience. Remember, all psychedelics except for ketamine are still illegal in the USA. It is a tricky area. If I were a patient, I wouldn't work with anyone who hadn't had at least ten psychedelic journeys themselves with the medicine they intend to serve me. I want them to know the landscape. I want "my" facilitator to trust the treatment.

Trusting the Medicine to Create Safety

In the Know Thyself section above, we discussed the importance of having direct experience with the medicine we serve. This allows us to develop an understanding of where our clients can go in their journeys. This expertise helps us build trust in psychedelic medicine. It takes a while for those of us with highly fortified, intellectual protector parts to open up to the idea that each psychedelic drug has its inherent wisdom and, with each psychedelic journey, its intention for what the journeyer is to learn.

The practitioner's trust in psychedelic medicine is evident when they hold space for someone. If someone is struggling, we offer support but understand at our core that struggle may be an essential process. We don't gloss over the challenge and pain of a "bad trip." Experiencing negative emotions moves us past the blocking energy of that emotion. If we are inexperienced and fear psychedelic medicine, we may inadvertently pathologize the experience and preemptively intervene and interrupt the process of allowing the emotion to make its way through the journeyer's experience in its wise way of healing.

Understand the Legality of Psychedelics

"Psychedelics are illegal not because a loving government is concerned that you may jump out of a third story window.
Psychedelics are illegal because they dissolve opinion structures and culturally laid down models of behaviour and information processing.
They open you up to the possibility that everything you know is wrong."

—TERENCE MCKENNA

At the time of writing, psychedelic medicines are, for the most part, still illegal in most of the world. In the USA, federally, all classical psychedelics are still considered Schedule I, even though ample scientific research has proven their incredible value as a class of psychiatric medicines. According to the DEA website: "Schedule I drugs, substances or chemicals are defined as drugs with no currently accepted medical use and a high potential for abuse. Some examples of Schedule I drugs are heroin, lysergic acid diethylamide (LSD), marijuana (cannabis), 3,4-methylenedioxymethamphetamine (ecstasy), methaqualone, and peyote."

Psychedelics are all illegal in the USA except for ketamine, which is listed by the DEA as a Schedule III medicine. According to the DEA: "Schedule III drugs, substances, or chemicals are defined as drugs with a moderate to low potential for physical and psychological dependence." Licenses in each state within the USA and other countries dictate who can provide psychedelic medicines for aboveground use. To administer ketamine, a person must have a Schedule III license. Approved healthcare providers include nurse practitioners, nurse anesthetists, physicians, psychiatrists, and in some states, naturopathic physicians.

Underground psychedelic practitioners vary in knowledge, training, and skill level. Most underground facilitators do not hold healthcare licenses. If they are licensed under current laws (except for Schedule III ketamine and FDA-permitted research studies), they are not operating legally within their healthcare license if they provide psychedelic medicines. Know your local laws and brush up on the specifics and ethics around the scope of practice of your particular licensure.

Collaborations with Medical Professionals and Psychotherapists

Many psychedelic facilitators, both aboveground licensed healthcare providers and underground facilitators, are not adequately trained to handle material that may emerge as part of a psychedelic experience. Appropriately qualified and experienced facilitators are less common than those who are not formally trained in psychology, and many don't know how to handle PTSD or complex trauma that often emerges during a psychedelic experience. I cannot express enough how essential it is to be expertly trained in trauma or collaborate with a therapist who understands the trauma territory.

Additionally, at the time of writing, if you are a therapist or psychologist who understands trauma but does not hold a Schedule III DEA license, you must collaborate with a licensed medical provider who has these credentials and will provide the medication for your patients. It is advised to have the medical provider in session with you so they may take vitals and administer medical interventions if necessary. Check your specific licensing rules, code of ethics, and scope of practice for your state license board. Psychedelic therapy is rapidly changing; more changes are likely as the field becomes increasingly mainstream.

Beware the Seduction of the "Guru Syndrome"

In the ninth century, the Buddhist sage Lin Chi told a monk, "If you meet the Buddha on the road, kill him." He meant that those who think they've found all the answers in any religion must keep questioning. The Buddha would neither profess nor try to convince others of his enlightenment, for this would imply he is compelled by an inflated ego in need of external validation.

Likewise, one of the biggest threats to the credibility of psychedelic medicine is that bad actors see the opportunity to seize upon the vulnerability and suggestibility of the journeyer. As the psychedelic field blossoms, professionals must recognize the importance of remembering who and why we serve (that is, our clients). I've met many people involved in medicine, technology, pharmaceuticals, and venture capitalism in the psychedelic industry. Even though sometimes there is finger-pointing, I haven't met one who doesn't think they're one of the "good ones," and no one realizes they might be a "bad guy." We witness the carving out of territory in the big money and land-grab of psychedelics, and some want to be the solitary gatekeepers of these medicines. Plant medicines evolved on this planet long before humans arrived. Others claim to know who should control the psychedelic field and how we should do things—whether licensed, fully legal practitioners, differentiated factions within, or the unregulated and underground folks. Magic dissolves when we lose curiosity and openness, replacing them with competitiveness, rigidity, fear, and exclusion.

The medicine, the sitting, and the holding are what matter. But ensuring proper scalability, accessibility, and safety is a huge conundrum. Humans often lose sight of our duty to help each other. Check in with desires and heal those parts desperate to feel necessary, powerful, and seen. When I pull the lens back, I recognize these characteristics as driven by the fear of being left behind or left out.

And then, there's the work of actually doing psychotherapy. It's often not glamorous. I recall sitting with a terrified client in her first ketamine-assisted psychotherapy (KAP) session. She'd had years of childhood abuse and was with an abusive partner. She had decided she was leaving, finally. I offered my Hero's/Heroine's Journey invocation, the music my business partner, David Starfire, produced, and the invocation I wrote and read. I offered an invitation to recognize her inner compass. She cried for the first hour, deep in the process. I sat, brought to tears myself many times. Often archetypal content arrives with various specificities—she had powerful visions of going into a cave, saying goodbye to the old life, and crawling on hands and knees back toward the light.

I recognized that archetypal path. I've done this same crawling in various ways, perhaps not as dramatically. The client sent me a message the next morning about how wonderful and amazing it all was. She declared, "You are a medicine woman and a sorceress!" We project our brilliance upon others when we can't see or accept it within ourselves. It isn't me creating the healing; I'm midwifing the psyche. She is seeing her own medicine. The magic is her sorcery, not mine. This process reorients me to my passion for the work and my *why*, which is to empower people to understand their own magnificence. I share this story to illustrate the seduction of grateful clients' often effusive gratitude and the attribution of the power of the psychedelic and the healing that follows onto practitioners. Don't allow them to lionize you; stay humble and in service to healing.

It is an honor and privilege to be trusted to witness and hold space for someone journeying in the psychedelic realms. These medicines are potent, nonspecific amplifiers. Before I used psychedelics in my practice, the trauma tools I used were akin to having a toolbox containing a handheld screwdriver and a hammer. When I added ketamine to my tool kit, it was like having a power drill and a pneumatic nail gun. We could accomplish much more in less time. But with power comes responsibility. A power drill and pneumatic nail gun can get work done faster and more efficiently, but they can also cause much more damage!

Recently, more awareness was brought to light surrounding guru syndrome. Documentaries like *Wild Wild Country* (2018) and *Bikram: Yogi, Guru, Predator* (2019) raise awareness about predators who exploit people who project god-like powers onto them. Practitioners who desire domination and worship are drawn to accessing vulnerable people through psychedelics. Please educate yourself and your therapy clients about being wise to the potential for abuse.

Patients are incredibly vulnerable while they are on the journey. Keeping them safe, honoring boundaries, and checking in with our parts are vital. Please read the section on consent in Chapter Seven. Many psychedelic journeys are so powerful and healing that clients often emerge overwhelmed with love and appreciation for the facilitator. Be cautious in receiving appreciation while managing this transference from clients. It is easy to become the recipient of projections like a guru, healer, or shaman. The projections get thrown out and then attached all too easily without the context of what those titles mean. They can easily tap into and activate our narcissistic parts that desire power and fame.

A genuine facilitator understands that healing doesn't come from them but rather from a higher source or the journeyer's innate healing intelligence. The more we can get our needy parts out of the way and allow Self energy to emerge, the more we can plug into and channel authentic healing energy. We are not the Source but rather a conduit of Source energy—whatever that means to the person we are assisting. I have had the honor of knowing many incredible healers and medicine people who are all humble. These folks make statements like, "I am a student of the plants," "I open myself to the guides, and they move through me," and, "Each person is already healed. I am only here to remind them of their radiance."

I have also met many people who insist they are shamans, priestesses, and medicine men. They say, "I drank ayahuasca last week for the first time, and it told me I am a healer and should start hosting ceremonies," and, "The person was resistant, so I told them they need to take more medicine." These dangerous narratives do not come from a place of integrity, expertise, or consent.

The litmus test is whether or not the facilitator makes the journeyer feel empowered and communicates that they trust each person has the wisdom to heal inside of them. A great therapist or facilitator helps clients access and then empower their Self energy. With confidence in the internal ecosystem, people depend on their own Self-leadership rather than an external source of Self energy. It is normal for therapy clients to initially rely on their therapist's Self energy as a modeling example of Self-leadership they may not have had access to as children in their families of origin. Great therapists recognize this and assist clients in using this external scaffolding to access their own internal Self-leadership, find ways to unburden the parts, and regain trust in Self energy to lead. This process is how the internalization of the locus of control occurs. It can also repair attachment wounds from early ruptures caused by caregivers who could not lead with Self energy. Great therapists support their clients' independence.

A few questions to ask when beginning to work with a therapist/facilitator are:

- Does the therapist continually ask for consent about touch, frequency of appointments, dosage of psychedelic medicine, etc.?
- Does the therapist consistently behave with integrity, honesty, and humility?
- Is the therapist consistently curious about the client and staying current on how the internal system is unburdening and adjusting toward healing, rather than assuming they already know what is best?
- Are they curious about the client's feelings and inner experience rather than telling them how they should feel?
- Are they patient with the client's progress?
- Do they honor their client's individual spiritual and religious beliefs, or do they seem to have their own spiritual or scientific agenda?
- Are they trauma-informed and trained adequately in trauma support methods?
- Are they culturally competent and knowledgeable of the importance of adequately supporting therapy clients from diverse backgrounds?
- Does the therapist refer patients to other, more appropriate therapists when the client's needs or background are outside their expertise?
- Is the compensation the therapist requests fair and appropriate for their service?
- Do they welcome feedback about how to best support the client?
- Do they honor the client's boundaries, and are they explicit and clear with their own?

Over the years, I've recognized my clients have helped me grow and heal more than I have helped them. It's an honor to witness another's awakening. Let us remember why we are all working so hard to bring these incredible medicines to everyone who needs them.

Your Attitude Toward Your Client:
Establishing Rapport

We must trust in the inherent goodness of our clients. Wisdom is innate in the psyche and will move toward health and wellness. Everyone has Self energy, no matter how deeply buried. Try to locate this in your clients as soon as you can. A therapist's Self energy locates their client's Self energy. Therapists negotiate with the parts, allowing core Self energy to shine through the system. I love Pema Chödrön's quote, "You are the sky. Everything else—it's just the weather" (1996). It is easy to imagine the Self is the sky, and the parts are the weather. They burden, unburden, and change roles, but the Self, the sky, is always behind them. I hold this vision when working with clients. I trust the sky is always there, no matter how intense the storms are. Eventually, the sky is revealed as the clouds clear and the storms pass.

A deep appreciation of the client and their process is vital. Understand it is an honor to witness someone's self-awareness and awakening. Genuinely caring about our clients helps provide the secure attachment scaffolding that they eventually internalize to create a secure attachment to the internal ecosystem.

When I was a novice therapist, I would withhold warmth from my clients because I wasn't confident in my abilities. I was worried that expressing that I cared about them would make them dependent on me or think we were friends instead of therapist and client. As my expertise and confidence grew, I realized there was no need to be stingy with compliments and kindness. As I have done my own work, I have become warmer and more secure with my internal ecosystem. I can extend much more emotional kindness and generosity to my clients. This ability has been enabled because I am immaculate with my boundaries. I am clear about payments, being on time for appointments, paying for missed sessions, and not self-disclosing much about my personal life. I compliment their hard work in therapy, genuinely care about their well-being, and enjoy working with them. Sometimes I am moved to tears by their triumph over suffering, and I am not shy about displaying my care.

I remember one of the most meaningful sessions I ever had as a therapy client was when I was crying about a trauma event I was struggling with at my therapist's office. I raised my eyes to meet those of my therapist; her eyes were sparkling and full of tears as she smiled warmly. I felt like she "got it" and was with me, witnessing and showing genuine compassion for how much I was hurting. The interaction was the most healing moment in my therapy with her, not her words or special therapy techniques.

An excellent resource on creating charisma, warmth, and social connection is Vanessa Van Edwards' book, *Captivate*. Van Edwards explains the science behind what particular cues help build genuine rapport. The book is intended for people who want to learn ways of becoming more socially adept, but the concepts apply to therapists looking to build their skills in establishing rapport and attunement.

Checking Your Agenda

Walker, your footsteps
are the road, and nothing more.
Walker, there is no road,
the road is made by walking.
Walking you make the road,
and turning to look behind
you see the path you never
again will step upon.
Walker, there is no road,
only foam trails on the sea.

—ANTONIO MACHADO,
BORDER OF A DREAM: SELECTED POEMS

Focusing on mutually agreed-upon therapeutic goals is essential to keep therapy on track. As therapists, we hold a vision of our therapy clients being healthy, resilient, and at peace. However, our agendas may creep outside the scope of treatment plan goals. Psychedelic journeys and their processes often evoke mystical and spiritual experiences and create epiphanies about relationships and life goals that require flexibility in the plan. Self-led therapists respect these mystical experiences and offer reflection when journeyers relay them without infusing them with their own beliefs and values. This idea goes back to trusting the medicine and the inherent wisdom of the patient's psyche.

I encourage clients not to make significant life decisions, such as leaving jobs or religions, moving households, or ending relationships (unless they are abusive), for at least a month as they integrate their psychedelic experiences. If something is true, it will remain valid, and it seems, once the psyche has expanded, it doesn't tend to revert to ignorance. Psychological and psychedelic work is an ongoing process. It is a labyrinth of a path toward self-discovery. The path is made by walking, and there is no final destination.

Remain aware of the treatment plan, but stay flexible. Accept parts that emerge as the system feels safer and safer. Treatment will shift and change as the internal ecosystem is discovered and how parts work and interact is recognized. The process of relationship-building is dynamic with every part. Being easygoing and respectful helps hold space for self-discovery. Follow the parts' lead while maintaining Self energy in the therapeutic dyad.

Illuminating the Path for Clients

As a facilitator, I am holding a lantern to illuminate my clients' underworld. I do not walk the path for them, but I am a collaborator in shining a light and helping to illuminate the path toward wellness. We may take side roads that are dead ends or find shortcuts. I hold curiosity, patience, and playfulness in the process because I trust that the healing is in the process, not the destination. I imagine having one foot in the underworld and one foot in the material world. I hold the vision of well-being, but I trust the timing of the unfolding. Meet clients where they are; taking delight in their self-discovery is an energizing and gratifying way to do therapy work.

Creativity and Curiosity

I enjoy the creativity inherent in working with archetypes, IFS, and psychedelics. As mentioned previously, psychedelics are nonspecific amplifiers. They are unpredictable, qualitative, and open-ended. My therapeutic style is one of creativity and flexibility. If your therapeutic style thrives in predictable, linear, and structured processing with a template to follow, being a psychedelic therapist may not be your style. This modality calls for ample creativity and curiosity.

In looking at psychedelic therapy through the lens of IFS, the medicine temporarily puts the protector and manager parts to sleep during the journey. These protectors must give consent to the process, and as they come back online, the therapist works with the entire system of protectors and exiles to help them feel safe while the protectors were temporarily unable to be vigilant due to the effects of the psychedelic medicine. Avoid promoting backlash from protector parts. Protector backlash is detailed in future sections about applying the Theradelic Approach. We proceed to work with exiles with attuned respect and care, and in so doing, we can often access deeply buried exile parts.

I am continually awed and mystified by the creativity of my clients' journeys. The wealth of symbolic content that arises is impressive.

I was working with a client in a psycholytic ketamine therapy session. This process involves a psycholytic dose of ketamine and processing for two continuous hours rather than an inward, quiet experience of a middose ketamine journey. She was naive about Jungian psychology, but her trips were richly infused with archetypal imagery. James Hillman, Joseph Campbell, and C.G. Jung would have been slack-jawed had they been in the treatment room listening to the ornate archetypal content she relayed from her unconscious mind. We were working with IFS and tracking her well-fortified protector system. She suspected a very vulnerable exile, but we couldn't access her. I engaged in a slow-paced, respectful dialog using direct access with a protector of her system dressed like a knight in full armor and carrying a large, heavy sword. He was exhausted from keeping vigilant guard for many years and felt lonely and sad. I asked him to show us his world. The protectors had created tall, thick rock walls that blotted out the sky. I asked him if he would be willing to lead us around the fortress. He agreed, and we traveled along the wall for a few minutes. The client was quiet then, and I allowed as much time as we needed to walk around this fortress. I often let go of an agenda, and the client journeys quietly. I know a lot is happening, and I am present to listen and talk when they are ready. Suddenly, the protector pointed out a tiny window in the stone wall. He seemed surprised it was there. The window was interesting, as I had not prompted the protector, and spontaneously the fortress and the knight felt safe enough to allow us to peer through a tiny window to an inner courtyard. It was no surprise to find a young girl inside, alone and afraid. It was an exile abandoned long ago.

As we looked through the window, with the knight standing near us but allowing us to see her, we worked with the knight to befriend him and understand his concerns about letting go of his vigilance. The little girl came closer to us, and the window got bigger. Then, the client reported seeing a drawbridge next to the window, surprised that it opened to the courtyard. We proceeded to work with the young girl inside, and as we unburdened her pain, she became free to explore her world with a light heart and playfulness. Often, unburdened exiles become joyful children who love to play, create, and enjoy the world.

There were a lot of tears during this session, accompanied by powerful feelings of nostalgia, love, and compassion for this girl who had been waiting for someone to see her and rescue her from her loneliness and pain. I always ask that the clients' managers and protectors are informed of what has just happened once they are woken up. As my client began to emerge out of the low-dose experience, and her managers and protectors began waking up, we let them know about the session. They were delighted to be relieved of their job but wanted to stay close to the fortress in case the exile needed protection. We agreed this was acceptable and desired, and we appreciated their work to ensure everyone's safety.

I trust my clients' inherent goodness. When looking into someone's eyes, there is a feeling of seeing that inner star. Protectors, exiles, and firefighters may cover it, but it is always there. Diane Poole Heller offers a simple exercise for therapists to help repattern secure attachment in clients called Kind Eyes. This involves gazing at others with softness, curiosity, and generous eye contact. I imagine compassion and love pouring out of my eyes and bathing others in kindness.

Self of the Therapist to Self of the Client

When we as therapists can tap into our Self energy, the client can access it too and use it as a scaffolding to soothe their parts. The modeling of Self energy helps them access their Selves and facilitates unburdening.

In Internal Family Systems, Self energy is composed of the Eight Cs:
- Calmness
- Curiosity
- Clarity
- Compassion
- Confidence
- Courage
- Creativity
- Connectedness

We all have parts, and the goal is not to rid ourselves of them but to unburden them so they can help the internal ecosystem and relate well to others. We may also have many Self-like parts, Self-led managers, and Self-led exiles. The difference between Self-like manager parts and the Self is whether or not there is an agenda. The Self does not have an agenda; it just *is*, existing in its glorious and all-encompassing presence. Self-led parts trust in the Self's leadership. The Self acts as a conductor and infuses the parts with the Eight Cs. There is an open line of communication between the parts and the Self, and not dissociative, sealed-off insular parts or blended energy. Self energy feels like a flowing, nourishing river of support that moves freely through the system. At times, we may become blended with a part that doesn't trust the leadership of Self, but over time, we get more adept at noticing when this happens and bringing Self energy in to request the part unblend so that we may unburden.

Being in Self energy with clients is akin to parents modeling secure attachment to their children, which the child internalizes to their internal parts; it is therapy helping people create secure attachments within their inner ecosystems.

All the Eight Cs are essential to embody as Self energy. Perhaps the two qualities that are especially pertinent are curiosity and creativity. When working with clients in the psychedelic realms, holding a stance of open, patient curiosity and being creative and adept at shifting to meet the client where they are in their process are helpful ways to support them.

The therapist's Self energy helps create a scaffolding for clients to access their internal Self energies. As a therapist, ask your protector and manager to step aside and allow the Self to guide the session. As mentioned in previous chapters, this is easier said than done. We must have a lot of self-awareness, be adept at "parts detection," and sense which parts we are blended with. You can inform the client that they are blended with a part and take a moment to go inside and ask parts to step out to be more in

Self energy while working with the client. This honesty and integrity are usually appreciated by clients and build trust.

Working with Projections, Transference, and Countertransference

Therapists also must be aware of their countertransferences during psychedelic journeys. Psychedelic medicine sessions can open clients to vulnerable exiles. It is common for clients to project a parental transference onto the therapist due to this inherent quality of the psychedelic experience with a facilitator. Transferences can occur in all sorts of relationships and are common in therapeutic relationships. Therapeutic transference and projection is the process of a therapy client unconsciously transferring feelings about someone in their life onto the therapist. It is essential to understand transference when engaged in psychedelic psychotherapy, both from the client to the therapist and from the therapist toward the client. David Hart explains Jung's concept of individuation in this way: "Whatever is unconscious within us is first encountered in projection; the process involves the withdrawal of projection and the assimilation of its content into that conscious being where it belongs—our own. It involves the ever-growing admission of who we are" (Young-Eisendrath and Dawson 2008, 92).

Freud and Breuer (1895) originally developed the concepts of transference and countertransference in psychology. Since then, these ideas have been adopted by most forms of psychotherapy. Freud and Breuer described transference as the intense and unconscious feelings that can develop in therapeutic relationships and distort the patient's sense of reality (1895). Most therapeutic modalities recognize how therapists respond to patients' evoked reactions, and the interaction process can be either beneficial or harmful in therapy (Fuertes et al. 2013). Humans are adept at detecting patterns from the past to predict what may happen in the future. We tend to compare what is happening now based on our past experiences.

There are three categories of transference:
- **Positive transference:** Pleasant and positive aspects of past relationships are projected onto the therapist. Clients project that the therapist is caring, wise, and empathetic, which can facilitate therapy.
- **Negative transference:** Negative feelings are projected onto the therapist. While this can be harmful and block treatment, if the therapist recognizes and explicitly acknowledges this, it can be discussed and woven into treatment.
- **Sexualized transference:** A client feels attracted to their therapist. This transference can include feelings of intimacy, sexual attraction, reverence, or romantic or sensual emotions.

Therapists can gain insight into a client's projections if they can identify when it is happening and explore it together. Transference can be welcomed with curiosity, articulated in therapy, and woven into therapy processing.

Sometimes, our clients can evoke countertransference, and our own exiles get triggered and blend with us. This process invites protector parts to rush in and rescue us from the perceived offender. Countertransference can happen so insidiously that it is easy to remain unaware of the process and merely react. A way to develop the ability to track this in real time is to see an IFS or psychoanalytically trained therapist.

If caretakers have been unsafe in the past, these transferences can be therapeutic in having a corrective experience of benign vulnerability with a caretaker. Offering safety, care, and support for clients experiencing acute vulnerability can be healing. The therapist must be adept at processing shame if it arises in clients after their protectors come back online and criticize them for being vulnerable. Tracking countertransference issues, such as our propensity for caretaking, infantilizing, and/or rescuing, is essential. Dr. Bill Richards advises trainees in psychedelic-assisted psychotherapy to use the acronym WAIT when facilitating psychedelic journeys. WAIT stands for "Why Am I Talking?" and reminds us to ask ourselves this question before intervening during a client's trip. Take just a moment to check in with parts, their intentions, and motivations when you have the impulse to engage during a session.

Creating Secure Attachment by Proxy

Therapists can play a crucial role in helping patients develop a sense of security and attachment through the therapeutic relationship, often referred to as "attachment by proxy." This process involves the therapist creating a safe and nurturing environment that allows the patient to explore their emotions and experiences and develop trust and safety in the therapeutic relationship, an effective and safe transference, in other words. The therapist can help the patient feel seen, heard, and understood by providing emotional support, validation, and understanding, fostering a sense of security and attachment.

Traditional attachment theory focuses on the individual's attachment to outside figures. IFS views attachment as happening both outside of the individual as well as internally, as IFS also creates an internal attachment between Self and the parts. It differs from attachment-based therapies, where the attachment focus is between the external world, for example, therapist and exiles, and understands that secure attachment is ultimately created inside each individual.

Research has shown that the therapist's ability to create a secure attachment with the patient can be a powerful predictor of therapeutic outcomes. A study by Fonagy et al. (2002) found that the therapeutic alliance (the relationship between the therapist and the patient) strongly predicts treatment outcomes, regardless of the therapeutic modality used. Another study by Norcross et al. (2010) found that the therapeutic alliance is the most consistent predictor of positive therapy outcomes. We have an opportunity in psychedelic therapy to provide corrective attachment experiences with our attention, attunement, and consistent care.

Children internalize securely attached caregivers in healthy, secure homes and transfer this attachment to their internal parts system. They enjoy a sense of security, safety, and resilience within themselves. As mentioned before, many of our clients have attachment wounds. The child learns the external world is unsafe if their caregivers are inconsistent in their attunement and care. This sense of insecurity then becomes unconsciously introjected as a mistrust within themselves. The therapist providing secure attachment with confidence, attunement, and care to the patient creates an external scaffolding of safety and trust. Consistent, emotional generosity can then internalize over time. The client naturally internalizes the locus of control from the outer world to create a secure attachment within the internal ecosystem. Psychedelic experiences can potentiate the introjection of secure attachment when facilitated by a therapist who understands the value of secure attachment by proxy.

Not Giving Up; Being a "Hope Merchant"

An important concept of IFS is being a "Hope Merchant." This means that the therapist acts as a guide and a helper in the healing process by helping the client access a part of themselves that is optimistic about the future. By connecting with the Self, the client can access internal resources, compassion, and a sense of purpose and meaning. When a part doubts or resists change, the Hope Merchant offered by a therapist can help the client develop optimism, a vital aspect of the healing process, particularly in the face of traumatic experiences.

There is often a place where the client becomes stuck in genuinely believing and trusting in Self-leadership and resistance to release a burden. The Hope Merchant can be a valuable intervention in moments of mistrust within the system. Offer encouragement with confidence and clarity that the part can safely release its burden. When in session, continually check in with your own parts too. Make sure you are in Self-leadership so you can convey hope with authority and self-assured energy.

7

OVERVIEW OF INTERNAL
FAMILY SYSTEMS (IFS)

Internal Family Systems (IFS) is a therapeutic modality I often use in combination with psychedelic-assisted psychotherapy. Please note this chapter is not a replacement for formal training in IFS. The Theradelic Approach recommends all clinicians complete at least Level One IFS training through the IFS Institute.

First developed by Dr. Richard Schwartz in the 1980s, IFS is a psychotherapeutic model that understands the human psyche as a complex system of parts, each with unique needs, desires, and motivations. These parts organize around a central core, the Self, a source of wisdom, compassion, and creativity.

The Self is the organizing principle of the psyche and is characterized by the eight Cs: calmness, clarity, curiosity, compassion, confidence, creativity, courage, and connectedness. These qualities are innate to all humans and accessible through the process of "unburdening" extreme parts to access this inherent substrate. The Self is the source of healing and transformation; providing all parts access to it is one of the primary goals of IFS therapy. The Self also lacks an agenda and the constant presence behind all the parts.

Parts are valuable subpersonalities that we are born with. They can be forced out of their valuable roles into extreme roles by trauma and become organized around a particular belief or emotion from the trauma. These parts can be exiles, protectors, managers, or extreme protectors, called firefighters. Exiles are parts of the psyche that carry pain, shame, or trauma and are often hidden or suppressed. Protectors are parts that emerge to shield the psyche from pain or vulnerability. Managers are parts that control behavior and emotions to avoid discomfort or maintain safety.

There is a specific process in IFS therapy to help parts gain more access to Self energy and establish trust in Self-leadership within the internal ecosystem. The process involves the Six Fs and the Healing Steps, and it is a system of measures to "unburden" parts from their extreme roles and help them feel more freedom and ease. IFS is non-pathologizing and understands that people are complex systems of parts that may have taken on extreme or dysfunctional roles. It presupposes everyone has Self energy beneath any parts trapped in dysfunctional roles. IFS is respectful and consensual in that the therapist and one's guidance system negotiate with the parts. As Dick Schwartz says, "There are no bad parts." The goal of therapy is not to banish, kill, or rid oneself of parts but rather to assist them in unburdening.

The IFS model emphasizes the importance of working with protectors before accessing exiles. Protectors serve a valuable function in maintaining stability and safety in the psyche and can be allies in the therapeutic process. By developing a relationship of trust and compassion with protectors, therapists can access the underlying exiles driving the client's symptoms.

IFS therapy aims not to eliminate parts but to help them function harmoniously and integrate them to access Self energy. With access to leadership and trust in the Self, parts can relax and have fluid roles in which they feel free to express themselves. By cultivating a relationship of trust and compassion with parts, therapists can help clients develop a more coherent sense of Self and increase people's capacity for self-regulation and emotional intelligence.

Research has shown that IFS can successfully treat various psychological issues, including depression, anxiety, trauma, and addiction. Ongoing research confirms and expands its utility for addressing a variety of issues. One study explored the efficacy of IFS therapy in reducing symptoms of post-traumatic stress disorder (PTSD) in a sample of twenty-two participants. Compared to the control group, the group that received IFS therapy showed significant reductions in PTSD symptoms, depression, anxiety, and stress and improved self-compassion and self-esteem (Khalsa and Greiner-Ferris 2021). Another study explored the use of IFS therapy as an attachment-based intervention for clients with trauma. The authors present two case studies of clients who received IFS therapy and showed significant reductions in symptoms of depression, anxiety, and trauma. The authors suggest that IFS therapy may be helpful for clients with trauma-related attachment issues (Price et al. 2018).

By developing a relationship of trust and compassion with these parts, therapists can help clients heal from past traumas, increase their emotional intelligence, and cultivate a more coherent sense of Self. IFS is a valuable tool for therapists seeking to deepen their understanding of the human psyche and help their clients achieve well-being. Proper training in IFS is essential. The course, run by the IFS Institute, is several months long, and the experiential component directly explains the model and its effectiveness.

Key Concepts in IFS

Self

In IFS therapy, the Self is the core essence of a person and is inherently calm, compassionate, and curious. The Self is the source of wisdom and healing within a person, and it is the foundation of the therapeutic process in IFS therapy. The therapist guides the client in accessing and strengthening their Self, which in turn helps them navigate and heal their internal system.

The Self is different from the other parts of a person's internal system, such as protectors, managers, and exiles. These parts can become overactive and interfere with a person's ability to access their Self. In IFS therapy, the therapist works with the client to understand the different parts of their internal system so they can negotiate and develop a more harmonious relationship, ultimately leading to greater access to the Self.

The Eight Cs of Self

In IFS, Schwartz has identified eight essential qualities to cultivating a healthy Self, often called the "Eight Cs." By embodying these qualities, clients can develop a deeper connection to their Selves and become more capable of healing and growth. The Eight Cs are a set of principles that guide IFS therapy. Again, they are curiosity, compassion, courage, clarity, creativity, calmness, confidence, and connectedness. The Eight Cs are an essential aspect of the IFS therapy process, and therapists often work with clients to cultivate these qualities throughout the therapeutic journey. Dr. Jeanne Catanzaro has offered a ninth C, "choice."

The more people can embody Self energy, the happier they are and the more access they have to guides (parts that have knowledge and wisdom and can help in the healing process). These principles help therapists create a safe and supportive environment for their clients to explore and heal their internal parts.

Protectors and Managers

At the heart of the IFS model are the concepts of protectors and managers, which are crucial to understanding how the mind functions and how therapists can help their clients heal.

Protectors are parts responsible for keeping the person safe from perceived or actual harm. They can take many forms, including the inner critic telling a person they are not good enough and parts that push them to work harder and achieve more. Protectors can be workaholics, punishers, internalized critical parents, controllers, heroes, and others. They can be perfectionists who want everything to be just right or the caretaker who puts everyone else's needs before theirs. They can become hypervigilant and preoccupied with emotional or physical safety. They can also create problems when forced to take on extreme roles of controlling external and internal circumstances. Some protectors can dissociate from the rest of the system to protect more vulnerable parts from pain and overwhelm. When found, protectors are usually older in age, as they developed to protect vulnerable, younger exiles. Exiles, discussed in more detail below, are parts that developed in childhood and are exiled from conscious awareness because what they feel is overwhelming. The extremity of a protector's burden typically indicates the extent of the exile's trauma. Protectors can also create problems in relationships and daily lives by overseeing intimacy and communication.

Conversely, managers are responsible for organizing our lives and ensuring we meet our goals. Managers "keep the show on the road" and try to appear normal to the outside world. Their roles can be dutiful employees or parents, friends, the good daughter or son, the athlete, and other roles that manage the system.

The Healing Steps of the IFS model involve working with protectors, managers, and exiles to help them let go of their burdens and allow their desired roles to emerge. This unburdening process is crucial to healing and involves assisting clients in identifying and understanding the parts' roles in their lives. Unburdening is achieved by helping them to "unburden" the extreme functions they took on when they lost trust in Self-leadership.

The therapist begins the unburdening process by developing relationships with the client's protectors and managers, acknowledging and respecting their essential roles. Through self-discovery and exploration, clients learn to understand their protectors and managers better and identify how these parts may be holding them back. The compassion and curiosity from Self energy are a big step in the unblending process of helping to unburden managers and protectors.

Once these roles have been identified, clients work with their therapists to release unbalanced burdens in the system. This process can involve techniques such as "In-Sight" (turning attention inside to access parts), mindfulness, visualization, and role-playing exercises.

Through this unburdening process, clients can reconnect with their true Selves, characterized by curiosity, creativity, compassion, and the rest of the Eight Cs. As the Self becomes more present in the client's life, they can better navigate challenges, build fulfilling relationships, and align with their values and desires.

The concepts of protectors and managers are central to the Internal Family Systems model, and understanding them is critical to helping clients heal. By working with these parts of the Self and helping the person release their hold on the Self, therapists can help clients live more fulfilling, authentic lives.

Firefighters

Another key component of the IFS model is the concept of firefighters, which are extreme protectors of the system that arise in response to a perceived threat or trauma.

Firefighters are parts that act as emergency responders when the system is threatened or overwhelmed. They are often extreme in their protection of fragile exiles. They can take many forms, such as addiction, self-harm, or compulsive behavior. At the apex of the most intense firefighter burdens is suicidality. While these behaviors can be harmful, firefighters are convinced these extreme behaviors are necessary to protect the system from further damage. Even firefighters who are suicidal are paradoxically trying to rescue the exiles from pain by ending the suffering. Although often challenging for therapists and clients, it is essential to respect firefighters and understand that, at their heart, they're trying to help. Finding a path to feeling compassion and curiosity toward them is crucial to negotiating with them to be less extreme in their efforts.

Shaming, shunning, or trying to force them to go away only exacerbates the situation and adds fuel to the fire, making them even more punishing and severe.

In the IFS model, firefighters are critical parts of the system that serve a protective function. We all have a hierarchy of firefighters who stand by to rescue us if life becomes overwhelming. However, sometimes their behavior can cause harm to the individual and their relationships. Thus, it is essential to work with these parts to find more effective and healthy ways to protect the system. Therapists must work carefully and slowly with firefighters. Proceeding too quickly or bypassing the firefighters can lead to backlash from them and harm to the system and, therefore, the person.

The unburdening process, central to the IFS model, involves helping individuals identify and understand their firefighters' roles in their internal ecosystems. This process begins by developing a relationship with these parts, acknowledging their importance, and respecting their role in protecting the system. If the firefighters feel heard and understood, they can relax and become less extreme and reactive. Once the system rekindles inner trust, firefighters voluntarily give up their extreme behaviors.

As individuals gain insight into the functions of their firefighters, they can develop strategies to help these parts let go of their extreme behaviors and allow for more effective and healthy ways to protect the system. By working with their firefighters respectfully and compassionately, individuals can gain a deeper understanding of the underlying emotional wounds that led to the development of these extreme protectors. As these wounds are addressed, the need for firefighters to protect the system diminishes, allowing the individual to access their true Self and the fragile exiles the firefighters have been valiantly defending. Once these exiles are freed and accepted into the system, they release their burdens and find more harmony.

Remember, firefighters are extreme system protectors that can arise in response to past trauma and emotional wounds. While their behaviors may be harmful, they are critical in protecting the individual. Through the unburdening process and the development of healthier coping mechanisms, individuals can learn to release the hold of their firefighters and access their true Selves, leading to a more fulfilling and authentic life.

Exiles

Another central idea in the IFS model is the concept of exiles. Exiles are abandoned and shunned parts of the system that can hold painful memories and emotions. They are usually young and hold the experience of being left behind, unaccepted, or shamed. Like small children, they are desperate to be heard and understood, but the protectors have buried them in the unconscious to protect the system from their pain and suffering. They feel abandoned and hopeless. If the protectors, or even firefighters, cannot keep them locked outside of conscious awareness, they will escape, forcing the system to recognize them. When exiles escape into consciousness, they flood the system and can wreak havoc on the person. Escaped exiles can become overwhelming and frightening to the system in their desperate need for help and to be witnessed in telling their stories. In IFS language, the person becomes "blended" with the exile and loses connection to calm Self energy. The more traumatized the exiles, the more extreme the protection in a system. Every person has exiles. They develop when overwhelming and traumatic experiences occur that the individual could not process at the time. When these experiences are too overwhelming, parts of the Self can become disconnected and isolated, leading to feelings of shame, guilt, and worthlessness. It is interesting to locate these exiles trapped in the past where something harmful happened, and they are lost there, looping in a stuck time and place. It is incredibly relieving for exiles to be retrieved from the unresolved limbo in which we find them.

In the IFS model, exiles are understood as a valued part of the system that must be healed and integrated into the entire being. It is vital because these parts can hold important information about past traumas and emotional wounds, and their unhealed state can lead to ongoing emotional and behavioral problems.

The unburdening process involves helping clients identify and understand their exiles' roles. This process begins by developing a relationship with these parts, acknowledging their importance, and respecting their role in holding memories for the system, even if repressed. As the client gains insight into their exiles' functions, they can develop strategies to help these parts heal and integrate into the system. The process can involve various techniques, including unburdening and retrieving using visualization, role-playing, and other forms of creative expression.

By working with exiles in a patient, respectful, and compassionate way, individuals can gain a deeper understanding of the underlying emotional wounds that led to the development of these isolated parts. As these wounds are addressed, the exiles can begin to release their hold on the system, allowing for a more integrated and balanced way of life for these parts.

Guides

Guides are a fundamental aspect of the IFS model, serving as a crucial resource for clients in their journeys toward healing and self-discovery. In *No Bad Parts*, guides are defined as "internal parts that have achieved a high level of healing and wisdom" (Schwartz 2020, 57). These guides are experienced as separate, distinct entities within the client's internal system, possessing unique qualities and strengths that can be called upon to assist the client in navigating their emotional landscape.

One of the primary benefits of working with guides is that they can provide a sense of safety and stability for clients, particularly those who have experienced trauma or other forms of emotional distress. By tapping into the wisdom and perspective of their guides, clients can access a greater sense of clarity and groundedness, allowing them to navigate their inner worlds better.

In addition to providing emotional support, guides can also be instrumental in helping clients achieve their goals and aspirations. As detailed in *No Bad Parts*, "Guides can help the client understand the purpose of their existence, the path they are meant to follow, and the steps they need to take to achieve their goals" (Schwartz 2020, 61). By collaborating with their guides, clients can develop a greater sense of purpose and direction.

Working with guides allows clients to cultivate greater self-compassion and acceptance. Access to guides reminds us that all parts are valuable and deserving of love and respect, and clients can develop a more positive relationship with themselves and their inner worlds. Connection to guides can benefit those who struggle with self-criticism or shame, allowing them to access a greater sense of self-worth and self-esteem.

Burdens and Unburdening

IFS provides a way for a client to release old beliefs, traumas, and extreme coping strategies that no longer serve them. The process for doing so is called unburdening. Unburdening involves releasing emotional burdens and unhelpful beliefs stored within the client's internal system. Burdens cause emotional distress and limit the client's ability to be present, spontaneous, and enjoy life. IFS states, "Burdened parts hold painful emotions and beliefs that interfere with the person's ability to function effectively" (Schwartz 1995, 27). Many experiences, including trauma, neglect, and unmet emotional needs, can cause these burdens.

The unburdening process involves working collaboratively with the client's internal system to identify and release these burdens. As detailed in *No Bad Parts*, "Unburdening is a process of accessing the wisdom and healing resources of the internal system to release burdens and restore balance" (Schwartz 2020, 122). This process is facilitated by the therapist, who works to create a safe and supportive environment.

By releasing these burdens, clients can access a broader range of emotional experiences, allowing them to live more fully and authentically. Additionally, the unburdening process can lead to a greater sense of self-acceptance and compassion, as clients can release the self-judgment and criticism that often accompany emotional burdens.

Another key aspect of the unburdening process is that it allows clients to heal from past traumas and emotional wounds. By accessing their internal systems' wisdom and healing resources, clients can work through these painful experiences and develop greater resilience and strength. This process can be constructive for those who have experienced complex trauma, allowing them to address the underlying emotional wounds.

For therapists looking to incorporate the IFS model into their practices, the books *Internal Family Systems Therapy* and *No Bad Parts* by Richard Schwartz provide a comprehensive overview of the unburdening process and its application within the therapeutic setting.

In-Sight, Direct Access, and Explicit Access

In the book *Internal Family Systems Therapy*, Richard Schwartz offers a comprehensive guide to the theory and practice of IFS. Drawing on decades of clinical experience and research, he provides practical tools and techniques for working with clients using the IFS model. Similarly, in *No Bad Parts*, Schwartz explores the concept of "parts" in depth and offers insights and strategies for working with challenging parts in therapy.

IFS offers a robust framework for understanding and transforming our inner worlds. Through cultivating in-Sight, direct access, and explicit access, people can begin to heal and integrate various parts.

In-Sight

"In-Sight" refers to becoming aware of and understanding our internal landscapes. This involves learning to observe and identify our different parts, as well as the patterns and dynamics that exist between them. Through gaining insight into our inner world, we can begin to make sense of our thoughts, feelings, and behaviors and develop greater compassion and understanding for ourselves.

Direct Access

Another vital aspect of IFS is the idea of "direct access," which involves the therapist connecting with a part in a direct, experiential way when a client cannot unblend from that part. The therapist asks to speak with the part directly and requests the part use the client's voice to communicate. This process allows parts to express themselves without judgment or suppression. Through direct access, the system can get to know the parts, build a deeper relationship with them, and learn to communicate and collaborate more effectively.

Explicit Access

IFS also emphasizes the importance of "explicit access," which involves actively engaging with parts consciously and intentionally. The therapist openly communicates that they will talk to the parts in the client's system. This method includes learning to communicate with parts, asking them questions, and seeking to understand their needs and motivations. Through explicit access, we can build trust and cooperation between our parts, work toward integrating them, and provide access to Self-leadership.

Applying the IFS Process

The Six Fs

The Six Fs of the unburdening process is key to the IFS approach. Therapists go through this step-by-step process to help clients unburden parts that feel overwhelmed, disconnected, or exiled.

The first F is Find and involves identifying the part causing distress. Therapists can help clients focus inside, track which parts are present, and begin to access their energy in somatic (physical) sensations, emotions, thoughts, auditory phrases, memories, and/or visual representations or memories.

The second F is Focus, which involves tuning into the bodily sensations associated with the part. Therapists can invite the part to increase the feeling so the client can understand the part's energy.

The third F is Feel Toward. The therapist inquires how the client feels toward the part. "How do you feel toward …?" is a question that helps determine how blended the part is with the person. If the answer is critical of the part or any feeling other than one of the Eight Cs, the therapist encourages the part to step aside. Often other parts step in and prevent Self energy from coming through in how the person feels toward the part. This step can take time, as clients are encouraged to keep asking for parts to step aside and unblend. At times, the therapist must even change the course of the therapy session to work with the manager and protector parts that have moved in and obscure the original part with which the contract was made. There is a saying in IFS: "Go slow to go fast." This is particularly relevant in the third step.

The fourth F is Flesh Out, which involves allowing the part to tell its story. Asking what it wants the client to know about it, its role, and how it is feeling are questions posed once the client has offered compassion and curiosity toward the part. The part may now feel safe to allow its story to be told.

The fifth F is beFriending, encouraging the client to extend Self energy to the part. This step involves cultivating a relationship of trust and compassion with the part, sending the part Self energy of care and connectedness, compassion, and curiosity. The therapist asks if the part senses the client's presence and if the client wants to get closer to the part to comfort them. This step involves a tender dialogue of care between the part and the Self with prompts from the therapist.

The final F is Fears and Concerns. It involves addressing concerns the part has about letting go of its role. This step involves increasing trust and getting permission to go deeper. We discover what the part fears in releasing its role and burden that serve the system.

The next phase of treatment is moving through the Healing Steps, which release the burdens of the protectors, managers, and exiles and integrate them into the larger system.

The Healing Steps

The Healing Steps of IFS involve identifying and working with the different parts of the client's personality to unburden them and allow more leadership from the Self. According to IFS therapist Ann Sinko, the first healing step is to unblend. Unblending means creating a critical mass of Self-to-part connections. Once this occurs, the therapist asks if the parts can step back and check how open the heart is to the part. Therapists directly ask how the client feels toward the part and listen for one of the Eight Cs in the answer (Sinko 2019).

The second step is to build a trusting relationship between the exile and the Self. At this step, slow down the process and take your time. Check the part's proximity and ask if the client can get closer. Send caring, compassionate energy from the Self to the part (Feel Toward step in the Six Fs). Ask if the part knows who the client is. It is vital to ensure the part is updated regarding the client's age, so inform them they are now "grown up."

The third step is witnessing, in which you ask the part to show and tell clients everything they need to understand about the past. The part may show scenes or convey feelings and sensations. Regularly check with the client that the level of emotion is tolerable. Process and continue to ask, "Is there more?"

The fourth step is retrieval, if necessary. The therapist asks if the part is stuck in the past. If it is, the therapist asks the part if it wants to come to the present with the client. If the part does not want to leave the past, the therapist inquires about their fears and concerns about leaving. It may be necessary for the Self to be with the part in a way that caregivers were not when the event initially occurred. Being with them means for the client to imagine themselves near the part, holding or hugging them. The therapist must ask the client to see what the part wants and obtain consent from the exiled part to hold them, soothe them, or take care of them in some specific way (brushing hair, singing a lullaby, playing with toys, showing the client around the scene, etc.) Sometimes the part wants to have a "do-over." A do-over means to replay the scene with the client's adult Self and the young part to protect the exile from what happened in the past. They may want the Self to rescue them from a scary place, confront an abuser, or help them run away. Notably, it is common to discover legacy burdens at this step. Legacy burdens are covered in more detail later.

The fifth healing step is unburdening. Unburdening happens when the therapist asks the client if they are ready to unload emotions or beliefs they took on from their experiences. If the part answers "Yes," the therapist asks the client to help the part take the burden out of their body and give it to the elements of fire, air, light, earth, or wind. If not, the therapist has the client ask the part about their fears and concerns and address them. We may also discover legacy burdens at this step.

The sixth healing step is an invitation. The therapist asks the part what qualities it would like to invite in, which ones it may need in the future, or what qualities are pushed out by the burden.

The seventh step is integration. The therapist invites the protective parts who stepped back earlier to witness the unburdening. Then the therapist welcomes the protectors to step back in and asks what roles they would like to have going forward. Do they want a new job? The therapist asks where the parts would like to stay.

The eighth step is intention. The therapist asks what the unburdened part wants from the client going forward and commits to checking in with the part to anchor the change in the system. It's essential to be sure the client agrees to continue building trust by checking in with the part.

The final step is appreciation. The client is invited to thank all the parts for showing up and working together for the good of the system.

Hope Merchant

As therapists practicing IFS, we play a unique role in helping our clients heal and integrate their inner worlds. A critical aspect of this role is serving as a "hope merchant," a source of encouragement, optimism, and possibility. The opportunity to offer hope can occur at any time in the IFS process. By offering hope to our clients, we can help them see the potential for growth and change and inspire them to take the steps necessary to achieve their goals.

Serving as a hope merchant involves recognizing and honoring the client's strengths and resources, as well as the potential for healing and transformation within their internal system. Being a hope merchant requires deep empathy, compassion, curiosity, and a willingness to explore and understand our client's unique experiences and perspectives.

IFS helps clients connect with their Selves, the compassionate and connected aspects of their beings. By cultivating a strong relationship with their Selves, clients can tap into their innate wisdom, strength, and resilience and find hope and inspiration in healing and growth.

Working with Polarizations

When working with parts, it is common to find deep-seated conflicts among parts with opposing agendas. Polarizations refer to conflicts between parts of a person's internal system that express as paradoxes or double binds. Polarizations can be revealed as therapists move through the Six Fs and the Healing Steps. These conflicts can manifest in many ways, such as a struggle between the desire for connection and the fear of vulnerability or between the need for control and the desire for spontaneity. These polarizations can create internal tension and may lead to difficulties in relationships or other areas of a person's life.

One of the key strategies for working with polarizations in IFS therapy is to help the client identify and access their Self. The Self can mediate between the different parts of a person's internal system, helping to resolve conflicts and bring balance and harmony. The therapist works with the client to cultivate a stronger connection to their Self, which can help reduce the intensity of polarizations and provide a greater sense of stability.

IFS therapists focus on helping the client better understand the different parts of their internal system and their inner relationships with each other. This strategy involves exploring the functions and motivations of each part and understanding how they interact. The therapist may use guided meditation, visualization, or journaling techniques to help the client explore their internal system more deeply. I like to have the client ask the polarized parts to come to a roundtable or a fire ring and encourage a dialogue between them. Eventually, we discover the polarized parts want the best for the system and are trying to help. Once we can extend Self energy to the polarized parts and bring in Self energy, the discussion becomes more productive, and the two parts find common ground.

Therapists can negotiate with internalized polarizations as if they are facilitating a nonviolent communication (NVC) process between two people. Developed by psychologist Marshall B. Rosenberg, this communication approach emphasizes empathy and honest expression of feelings and needs (Rosenberg 2003). NVC involves four key components: observation, feelings, needs, and requests. It encourages individuals to listen without judgment, express themselves in a way that does not blame or criticize others, and focus on the underlying needs and values behind their own and others' actions. By doing so, NVC aims to create understanding, connection, and cooperation between individuals in all types of relationships. Working with the internal polarized parts, the therapist can guide the client to encourage each part to observe, share feelings, state positive needs, and make requests of the opposing part.

The therapist may also use techniques such as unblending or externalizing to help the client work with polarizations. Externalizing involves helping the client view their parts as separate entities, which can reduce the intensity of polarizations and provide a greater sense of distance and perspective.

Working with Legacy Burdens

IFS acknowledges the impact of cultural or family trauma on individuals through the concept of legacy burdens. Legacy burdens are unresolved issues or traumas from previous generations or culture. These burdens may be partially carried within an individual's system but are mostly or entirely from parents, grandparents, and ancestors.

Letting go of legacy burdens is an integral part of the IFS process, as it allows a release of patterns and beliefs that may hold a person or a group back in frustrating and confusing ways. The process involves connecting with the parts of ourselves that carry legacy burdens and offering them the support and compassion they need to heal.

One way to release legacy burdens in IFS is during "exile retrieval." This process involves identifying the part carrying the burden and returning to the original trauma or experience that created it. Then, if the exile hesitates to release the burden fully, it may signal that a legacy burden needs to be removed. At that point in the process, the therapist and client may discover a legacy burden, and the therapist can assist the client in sending back the burden through the generations to where it originated. By offering compassion and understanding to this ancestor, we can help it release the burden through the lineage and integrate it into the client's system.

An essential approach to offloading legacy burdens is maintaining "Self energy," as well as the therapist serving as a hope merchant, especially if the part or the ancestors has doubts about releasing such an immense or intense burden. Self energy is compassionate and connected and can hold space for all our parts, including those carrying legacy burdens. The Self can support and guide our parts and ancestors and help them release their burdens.

Working with Unattached Burdens

A lesser-known concept in IFS but one that a psychedelic-informed therapist should understand is unattached burdens (UBs). These malevolent energies are not internal parts of a person's system. They attach like parasites and extract energy while adding negative energy. These entities are found in many cultures and religions. Shamans, medicine women and men, patients, rabbis, priests, and therapists have encountered UBs throughout human history. Richard Schwartz discovered UBs by using IFS techniques with thousands of patients. Although they are rarely encountered, it is essential to familiarize oneself with them and have the necessary skills to free the person's system from harm.

Unattached burdens are not part of a person's internal ecosystem; they are energies from the outside. Interestingly, Schwartz discovered UBs can't lie, so the therapist can ask direct questions and get honest answers. Sometimes they are evasive, and the therapist must be tenacious in encouraging and questioning where they came from. The goal is to send them off to go back "into the light" or to where they originated.

Therapists should receive at least Level Two IFS training to work with more challenging issues like polarizations, legacy burdens, and unattached burdens.

In the next chapter, I will discuss how I weave IFS into psychedelic therapy sessions using the steps in the PANTHER method.

8

PANTHERS IN THE GOLDEN HOUR: KETAMINE-ASSISTED PSYCHOTHERAPY TREATMENT

The PANTHER method is an acronym that outlines the Theradelic Approach process of hosting a psychedelic journey. Therapists can use the PANTHER method to formulate client treatment plans and schedule the intake, preparation, medicine, and integration sessions.

The PANTHER method guides an idealized flow for a psychedelic journey from start to finish. Psychotherapy is both a science and an art and is a somewhat—but not entirely—predictable process. While keeping in mind that including every step of the PANTHER method is optimal in the Theradelic Approach, take comfort that it is acceptable to be flexible in treatment planning. Clients and therapists can be busy, and schedule conflicts often come up. Insurance may only cover some of the sessions, or the client may be unable to afford all the sessions that the therapist deems optimal. Getting people the treatment they need is essential, even when we cannot be perfect. That said, some aspects of the model are non-negotiable, such as consent and creating safety (i.e., therapists need to be trauma-informed). Other model components are more flexible, such as the number of preparation sessions before the medicine or the number of integration sessions scheduled after the journey sessions.

Before exploring PANTHER in more depth, it is crucial to understand the concept of "set and setting" for psychedelic journeys.

Set and Setting

Ludwig von Bertalanffy used the terminology "set and setting" as early as 1958. Popularized by Timothy Leary in 1961 through lectures and interviews, set and setting became widely accepted by researchers and therapists in psychedelic therapy. These terms are used frequently in psychedelic training programs today. "Set" refers to our mindsets when entering the psychedelic space, including thoughts, moods, and expectations. I would add that this "set" also involves what clients bring to the session, such as previous traumas, developmental stages (which may not equate to actual age), and neurochemistry. "Set" includes recent media, social interactions, food and drink consumption, and the corpus of the person's prior psychedelic and psychotherapeutic experiences. Being mindful of set and setting is essential because psychedelic medicines tend to extrapolate what the person has been thinking about or emotionally processing, what they have recently learned, and the media they have recently consumed. This content is often reconfigured and presented back to the journeyer in the imaginative interplay of the experience. Therefore, encouraging clients to become cognizant of how they discern their mindsets can be very helpful in curating the content of the journey.

"Setting" refers to the social and physical environment of the journey itself. Psychedelic researcher Al Hubbard introduced a "treatment space decorated to feel more like a home than a hospital," which came to be known as a "Hubbard Room" (Pollan 2018). The Hubbard Room improves the psychedelic "setting" to enhance positive outcomes. Unlike an austere hospital room, a Hubbard-style room is decorated in a neutral, warm decor and feels comfortable.

Designing the Treatment Protocol

The timing and frequency of medicine sessions vary with each psychedelic medicine, but the PANTHER steps remain consistent regardless of the medicine. Because ketamine is the only fully prescribable psychedelic medicine at the time of writing, we will discuss protocols for it.

Preparation therapy sessions follow the initial intake visit. The standard of the initial intake is the same as regular non-psychedelic psychotherapy. If the client is an appropriate candidate for KAP, the subsequent session(s) are for preparation. These are fifty to sixty minutes long and are generally scheduled a week apart. Sometimes more preparation sessions are required to allow time for proper trauma mapping, rapport-building, creating safety, and providing IFS therapy to support access to Self energy before a medicine session. Add as many preparation appointments as necessary, as discussed below.

Once the preparation is complete, schedule the ketamine-dosing appointment. Ketamine appointments range from two to three hours, depending on the dose and route of administration. Orally administered ketamine metabolizes more slowly than intramuscular injection. Middose sessions are longer than psycholytic (low-dose) sessions. Each person's metabolism is different as well. Generally, because no one knows beforehand how the client will metabolize the medicine and how long to schedule the session, I schedule the initial journey with an hour of buffer time at the end of the day if the session exceeds the allotted time. I generally plan two hours for psycholytic sessions and three hours for middose sessions.

I schedule ketamine sessions one or two weeks apart, with at least one integration session between the medicine sessions. Sometimes more integration sessions are appropriate before another ketamine session. Again, this allows for proper metabolism of the content of the experience.

Ketamine is a promising intervention for individuals who have not responded to traditional antidepressant treatments. However, the optimal frequency of ketamine therapy remains unclear. Several studies have investigated the optimal frequency of ketamine therapy for treating depression. A randomized controlled trial conducted by Fava et al. (2020) found that individuals who received weekly ketamine infusions for four weeks experienced significant improvements in depressive symptoms compared to those who received a single infusion. Similarly, a meta-analysis by Shiroma et al. (2014) found that six ketamine infusions over two weeks significantly reduced depression symptoms.

However, other studies have suggested that a less-frequent dosing schedule is optimal. A randomized controlled trial by Wilkinson et al. (2018) found that people who received a single ketamine infusion experienced significant improvements in depressive symptoms that lasted up to twenty-eight days. Another study by Singh et al. (2016) found that biweekly ketamine infusions resulted in sustained antidepressant effects for up to four weeks.

This demonstrates that a single protocol has yet to emerge as the ideal. More research is needed to determine the optimal frequency of ketamine therapy for various mental health diagnoses. Current evidence suggests that weekly or fortnightly ketamine infusions may be effective for treatment-resistant depression.

After three to six ketamine medicine sessions, with integration sessions interspersed between medicine days, schedule an integration appointment to explore how the client is feeling. This is a moment to evaluate the process if the sessions should be spaced further apart or discontinued for a time. Conclude treatment by scheduling a final appointment to discuss the treatment trajectory, how the client feels they have changed, and whether there has been a subjective improvement in their condition.

How Many Sessions?

Trainees often ask me how frequently ketamine should be given and at what dose. There is not one single answer. Clients have different mental health needs, physiologies, budgets, and availability. I generally encourage clients to receive at least three KAP sessions spaced one to two weeks apart. After three sessions, we can assess if more are needed and how far we can space sessions out. I have had clients experience an alleviation of depression and/or anxiety for a week or two and then need a maintenance session. I have also had clients who, after three sessions, had such life-changing experiences they felt changed forever and haven't felt called to have more ketamine experiences. Luckily, we have the latitude to be creative with this medicine.

I do not recommend giving ketamine more than twice a week for ongoing periods. This topic is hotly debated among KAP practitioners. Still, some studies indicate, when used in high doses or over an extended period, ketamine can cause several side effects, including interstitial cystitis (IC). IC is a chronic condition characterized by bladder pain, discomfort, pressure, and urinary frequency and urgency, which can be severe and debilitating.

The symptoms of ketamine-induced IC can be severe and lead to chronic pain and long-term damage to the bladder. A study published in *The Journal of Urology* in 2014 found that chronic ketamine users had a higher incidence of bladder inflammation, bladder wall thickening, and other signs of bladder damage. Another study published in *The Journal of Urology* in 2016 found that ketamine abuse can lead to IC-like symptoms, including bladder pain, discomfort, and urgency (Jhang et al. 2014). I know two people who suffer from ketamine-induced IC. Some experts dispute ketamine can cause IC. Hopefully, we will soon have more research to draw from because of the explosion in ketamine use over the past few years.

Weaving in Regular Therapy between Psychedelic Sessions

The psychedelic medicine session is only one component of effective therapy. Take time to prepare for the experience and integrate it fully. Sometimes it is not psychedelic medicine that is most helpful but rather good old-fashioned psychotherapy. Weave in regular therapy sessions as needed and keep the treatment protocol flexible to add sessions before, in between, or after psychedelic sessions. When clients have a profound psychedelic experience and rich integration afterward, they may not feel drawn to having another medicine session for an extended period.

PANTHER

The PANTHER steps flow throughout the treatment process. The P, A, N, and T (Preparation, Attunement, Needs of the protectors, and Trauma mapping) steps occur in the preparation phase of psychedelic treatment. The H and E (Hold space and Empathy and engagement) steps occur during the medicine journey, and the R (Resolution and integration) step happens during the integration phase.

A therapist can plan treatment and provide effective psychedelic therapy by remembering the acronym PANTHER.

PANTHER stands for:
- Preparation and intake
- Attunement
- Needs of the protectors
- Trauma mapping
- Hold space
- Empathy and engagement
- Resolution and integration

PANTHER is woven throughout a treatment plan as a sequence of steps to facilitate psychedelic therapy properly. Psychedelic treatment planning is meant to be flexible. All protocols for psychedelic therapy involve preparation, the journey itself, and integration. We will explore each step in more detail.

Preparation and Intake Appointments

A psychedelic experience with a facilitator is an emotionally intimate experience. The patient's vulnerability is more profound than in regular talk therapy. Having an attuned, well-trained, safe, and confident psychedelic therapist can be a profoundly healing experience. The delicate nature of the arrangement underscores the importance of establishing rapport, safety, and trust in the preparation phase of the process.

The intake appointment is an opportunity to sense the landscape of your client's internal and external worlds and build rapport. Taking a stance of curiosity and using non-pathologizing language helps to establish safety. It is best not to encourage clients to jump in and begin talking about trauma in the initial intake session. Sometimes people have told their trauma stories so often that they have become well-worn grooves in the brain, entrenched into the psyche, and separate from the actual event(s). Alternatively, people with exiles desperate to be seen and to feel a connection (common in those with disorganized attachment trauma) may offer trauma stories to bond with new people too quickly. Shame and remorse from punishing protector parts often follow the oversharing. If a client begins going into the trauma story in the initial appointment, gently offer that you believe them and redirect them to skip the details for now.

Prioritize understanding their attachment style: secure, insecure, anxious, avoidant, or disorganized. Daniel Brown's and David Elliott's book, *Attachment Disturbances in Adults: Treatment for Comprehensive Repair* (2016), helps develop treatment protocols and exercises to encourage secure attachment by proxy. Learning a client's attachment style takes time. Listen for specific chronic behavior patterns and relationship storylines that reveal attachment patterns. Begin to map out a trauma landscape of events, when they occurred, and any repetitive relational dynamics.

If it is the first time you have met the client, encourage them to book another appointment after they have had time to reflect upon your session.

I always explain that it is essential for them to be an informed consumer and feel a sense of compatibility with a new therapist. I encourage them to sense if they feel rapport and whether my therapeutic style and skill set are what they seek in a therapeutic relationship. I am direct and clear about my training and skills and what are not my specialty areas. I am explicit with boundaries about missed appointments, scheduling, and my fee structure. I have learned this creates an amicable, clear relationship from the start, allowing a better flow in the long run.

Consider whether this client is a good candidate for psychedelic-assisted psychotherapy during the intake appointment and the first few meetings. Err on the side of caution and screen out clients with active mania or hypomania, bipolar disorder, or those who have a history of mania, schizophrenia, or paranoia. These mental health concerns are not recommended for psychedelic therapy outside of studies. It doesn't mean psychedelics cannot help them, but there isn't enough current research or evidence to support psychedelic use for these mental health issues. Research is developing quickly, and it may be discovered that these disorders benefit from psychedelic-assisted psychotherapy.

Additionally, this therapy is not officially recommended for narcissism, borderline personality disorder, dissociative identity disorder, and antisocial disorders. I don't necessarily screen these people out of treatment; instead, I take more time preparing them for the medicine sessions. From the non-pathologizing IFS perspective, these issues are caused by a lack of access to Self energy, and a blending of protectors and exiles has obscured the Self. I recommend taking more time in the preparation phase with these populations to help clients access Self energy with IFS therapy before embarking on the medicine journey.

There has been some research into autism spectrum disorders with psychedelics and treatment for adolescents. Therapists can use their judgment in these cases. Unless you are involved with a research study, I recommend being conservative about recommending psychedelic treatment for populations outside the better-studied disorders of anxiety, depression, post-traumatic stress, and related disorders.

It's best to know the client's trauma history before proceeding with ketamine. Of course, unknown trauma episodes often emerge during psychedelic journeys. However, understanding attachment styles and known trauma events can help prepare clinicians and patients. It usually takes a few preparation therapy sessions to get a good sense of a client's history and to create safety and rapport to proceed with ketamine therapy. Taking time to prepare correctly saves time and effort in the end. Ultimately, the client heals in less time with less expense.

Another reason for performing adequate trauma mapping before dosing is that we can base the ketamine dosage on the client's history. For example, many patients who have experienced trauma have a freeze response when re-experiencing a similar situation. In higher doses, ketamine can make people feel like they cannot move their bodies and are numb and dissociated. This dissociation, in turn, can evoke trauma memories due to the aforementioned state-dependent processes. This new paradigm can become pleasant when adequate preparation has laid the groundwork to repattern the meaning of frozen dissociation to a pleasurable experience of relaxation and freedom. The new belief could become, "I am safe when I relax and let go," and can serve as a corrective experience to make vulnerability a safe experience.

Preparation for Psychedelic Appointments

The psychotherapist must prepare a client for a psychedelic therapy session by providing detailed information about the process and addressing any concerns or questions the patient may have. This process includes discussing the risks and potential benefits of the therapy. Explain what they can expect during a psychedelic session, such as the duration, setting, and any detailed instructions for preparation. You should also explain your role as a therapist during the session and what the patient can expect from the experience, such as the potential for heightened emotions, insights, and new perspectives.

Work with your client to establish clear therapeutic goals for the session and to identify any specific issues or areas of focus for the therapy. Preparation includes the client setting an intention for the session and being open to the potential for new insights and emotional breakthroughs. Explain how they can integrate the experience into their daily life and continue with therapy after the session.

There are a few specific preparations that the Theradelic Approach uses before the medicine session.

Music

We discuss the music we will play, and I ask the client to bring a pair of headphones. Music is an essential healing element of the psychedelic experience and influences the journey.

Explain the importance of listening to unfamiliar music with unrecognizable or no lyrics to your client. Unfamiliar music helps create new experiences. If the song is known or the lyrics understood, it can take the experience in a specific direction that may take the journeyer off the path of their process and in a direction informed by the music. I encourage clients to listen to their own music playlists if they know what is required to make beneficial psychedelic playlists. I do share my music playlists if requested before the medicine session. I am quite discerning in my musical taste, so I understand when clients inquire about being able to listen to the playlist before the session.

Sometimes clients like to listen to the playlist after the session in the following days during the integration phase. I encourage this, as it often helps them recall details of their journeys. This practice seems to extend the longevity of the benefits of ketamine therapy.

Therapists can find many playlists already created on popular music platforms, or they may create their own. I am passionate about creating custom playlists because music greatly influences the psychedelic experience. I feel that music as a co-therapist helps guide the journeyer through the landscape. In 2020, I started a company called PsyAssist with composer and music producer David Starfire. We have created meditations and music for psychedelic journeys. We were acquired by the virtual reality company TRIPP in 2021, of which I became the clinical director. Once a therapist hosts a few psychedelic journeys, they will better see how music carries the journey.

Logistics

Discuss logistics for the day of the medicine: what to wear (dress in comfortable layers, make upper arm accessible for injection site if applicable), and what to bring (pillows, eye mask, headphones). Cover what to expect on the day of the treatment. Explain what the medicine is like in terms of buildup, peak, and a long tail of returning to the ordinary mind.

Explain the duration of the medicine's effects and that nausea is uncommon (less than five percent and more common with lozenges) but is a possible side effect of psychedelic medicine. Get the name, relationship to the patient, and phone number of the person picking them up, and make sure they have arranged a ride home. They are not to drive on the day of the session after ketamine. Also, explain that they must fast for at least six hours before the session; they may drink coffee, tea, and water.

No ingestion of alcohol is to take place for two days before and two days after the session. Refraining from alcohol is important, not only because it is contraindicated for ketamine use, but also because abstaining from alcohol may encourage more neuronal growth and cognitive plasticity following the ketamine experience.

Some psychedelics are unsafe when mixed with most psychotropic medications. Ketamine is an exception because it binds to different receptors in the brain than classic psychedelics. If a patient takes certain psychotropic medications, my medical provider may instruct to withhold the medicine the morning of a ketamine session. Please consult with your medical provider for these specific instructions regarding prescribed medications. According to abundant anecdotal reports, many believe that grapefruit can increase the potency of some psychedelics, particularly LSD and psilocybin. If you are working with these medicines, advise your client to refrain from citrus fruits the day before the session and on the day itself. Monoamine oxidase inhibitors in some antidepressants and herbs may also have a potentiating and extending effect on tryptamine psychedelics, and care should be used.

Ground Rules

The ground rules are that the client agrees not to leave the area and not to become violent. Explain that you will only touch the client to offer a hand if requested and to assist should they be in danger or need assistance to go to the restroom. Explain that the medicine has an approximate duration of effect.

Sky Map

The Sky Map is given to the client to know what to expect from the medicine session. Explain that, no matter how far out they go on the journey, they will return to their ordinary mind and body awareness. Encourage clients to go to the restroom just before dosing, as it can be challenging to move around once the medicine sets in.

Advise clients to surrender to the experience as much as possible. Remind them to recall their intention as a positive rather than a negative statement. Many of us trained in psychedelic-assisted psychotherapy by the originators of the Western medical model were taught a common phrase intended to guide the journeyer as they begin their session: "Trust, be open, and let go." This may be a good mantra for many, but be aware that, for some people who have experienced trauma, the concept of trusting and letting go can be triggering. They may not have felt trust or safety enough to "let go and be open." Rather than forcing passivity in the experience, I offer journeyers to actively invite the medicine into their bodies, minds, and spirits as a collaborator. Encourage the client to coordinate healing with the medicine and ask it to help them. Explain it is like greeting a new friend and hosting them in the client's sacred space. Remaining physically still as they return to normal sensations in the body and ordinary mind helps clients remember more from their experiences. Rather than: "Trust, be open and let go," I prefer: "Be curious, be centered, and just ask."

After they return from the journey, invite your client to lie quietly, go over the journey, and try to anchor at least three things into their memory about what they experienced, saw, heard, and felt so that they can remember as much as possible. Recalling the journey material is not a necessary step to receive benefits from the experience, but it can help to amplify the healing process. In the case of ketamine at low and midrange doses, remembering the journeys is similar to recalling dreams. When we wake from a dream, lying quietly and recalling it with as much detail as possible creates a lasting memory. If we get up and move around straight away, we tend to forget the dream. The higher the dose of ketamine, the less information clients tend to be able to recall.

Setting an Intention

Setting an intention for a psychedelic experience is crucial because it helps to focus the mind and allows the individual to clarify their goals and objectives for the session. It provides a sense of purpose and direction for the journey. It can also increase their chances of having a beneficial and meaningful experience by directing their attention and energy toward what is most important to them. Setting an intention can also enhance the therapeutic benefits of the psychedelic experience by providing a framework for understanding and integrating any insights or breakthroughs that may occur. Additionally, setting an intention can reduce anxiety by providing a sense of control, which can help to mitigate any adverse effects of the psychedelic experience.

One technique I often use to build intention is to remind the client of the Eight Cs of Self-leadership: confidence, calmness, creativity, clarity, curiosity, courage, compassion, and connectedness. I encourage them to bring each quality into their mind and explore which of the Eight Cs they can access and which ones they want to bring more of into their life. For example, clients may feel great about embodying creativity and confidence in their daily lives, but they lack connectedness to others because they feel isolated. The quality of connection becomes the intention. I encourage them to frame it in a positive statement, such as: "I am connected." Taking it a step further, I encourage them to put their positive intention into a symbol. Our minds tend to hold visual images and emotions better than words. Perhaps in the example of "I feel connected," the image could be a circle of people holding hands.

Another way to assist the client with an intention is to ask what they hope to get from the journey. Have them create one sentence—a simple, positive intention that can carry that meaning. Guide them to choose a visual symbol to hold the intention. For example, a client under a lot of stress at work might say, "I don't want to be so stressed out all the time!" Ask them to restate it as a positive statement, such as, "I want to feel peace." Then, ask them to choose a symbol, such as a dove, to remind them of their intention on the journey if they get disoriented or lost.

Managing Expectations

The media's excitement about a new treatment option has painted a heady picture of psychedelics being a cure-all, with dramatic reports of one treatment ending someone's mental illness forever. Psychedelic medicines are not a panacea. While they can improve symptoms, they do not tend to cure people of mental illness after a single treatment. It is essential to be clear and realistic and manage patients' expectations. If a client is desperate and implores you to administer the ketamine treatment immediately, this is a red flag. Be cautious. Clearly explain the importance of all the therapy before, during, and after the psychedelic medicine dosing. The entire therapeutic process is what amplifies the power of the medicines.

Sometimes clients come to see us after they have exhausted every other option they could think of. Understandably, they hope the psychedelic will finally cure their suffering. Many clients come with unrealistic expectations. A single psychedelic experience rarely results in the complete remission of depression, anxiety, or PTSD. Although I have seen miraculous results with ketamine therapy, rarely have I seen it cure a person after only one experience. Sometimes clients may feel frustrated the journey didn't go as they had hoped. The material was bleak, different from what they wanted; they had a "bad trip," or their intention may not have come up in the journey. Keep an attitude of curiosity around even the most void or dismal visions clients may have because this theme may be an entry point for further insight and downstream integration.

It is essential to manage expectations with the client before the medicine day. I often repeat, "There are no ways to do it wrong and every way to do it right." Ask them to hold their intention loosely and be open to whatever comes up. After witnessing hundreds of journeys, I trust there is wisdom in the process, and the medicine will take people where they need to go. It might not make sense right away, and sometimes the material revealed is more than the client is ready to see, but it is essential to be open and curious about the experience. The meaning we weave into our life stories is more important than whether they're pleasant or unpleasant.

Attunement

Attunement is one of the most important tools a therapist has during a psychedelic treatment session. With attunement, the therapist is acutely present in the moment and engaged in active listening. Attunement builds rapport and creates safety. Focus entirely on the client, pay attention to facial expressions, track emotion in the voice, and actively listen to the words. Practice deep listening to what is said and if it is coherent with the other cues. Watch body language and voice inflection. These are all ways of being attuned.

Research has shown that therapeutic attunement is an essential factor in the effectiveness of psychotherapy. According to a study by Fonagy et al. (2002), "the capacity to mentalize, or to reflect on mental states, is a crucial aspect of therapeutic attunement. The capacity to mentalize is associated with forming and maintaining healthy relationships, and it is thought to be a key mechanism of change in therapy." The study concludes that therapeutic attunement is a critical element of successful therapy. It helps create a secure and supportive environment for clients to explore their inner experiences and resolve their issues.

A famous quote, often attributed to Maya Angelou, sums up this idea of attunement: "I've learned that people will forget what you said, people will forget what you did, but people will never forget how you made them feel." Attunement helps people feel as if they matter. It helps therapists coregulate clients by tracking their emotional energy and adding calm, Self energy.

Needs of the Protectors: Obtaining Permission

Before you offer ketamine, explore specific protector parts that have developed in clients with trauma histories. These important protectors develop elaborate ways to manage the system and help keep the overwhelming exiles from view. Protectors must be honored and appreciated by both the therapist and the client. Rushing in too soon to a medicine session can backfire. Ketamine and other psychedelics tend to suppress activity in the default mode network, where the psyche's system managers and protectors reside.

Suppose we temporarily put these managers to sleep without obtaining their consent. The psychedelic may allow vulnerable exile parts to be accessed while the drug is active. What happens when the forced-out protectors "wake up" and come back on duty without having agreed to the exiles being exposed? There is commonly a backlash once the protector parts return online after the psychedelic experience. This experience may cause your client to feel vulnerable and ashamed. Unprotected exiles may have needed help from the facilitator during the journey. Protectors have punished the exiles for requesting assistance in the past or for revealing secrets that are forbidden to be shared.

Consent from Protectors

I explicitly ask if any parts do not feel comfortable working with psychedelics before proceeding. I take all the time needed to ensure patients and their parts are clear about what will happen, have all their questions and concerns answered, and have given consent before proceeding. The IFS refrain, "Go slow to go fast," applies here. In the preparation session, I offer a brief guided meditation to ask the protective parts how they feel about the upcoming ketamine session. I ask if they have any questions or concerns and take the time to address them.

Clinicians must obtain consent from the protector parts before proceeding with ketamine or other psychedelic sessions. Letting these parts know they will be temporarily asleep is helpful so the internal ecosystem knows what to expect. Once I obtain consent from all the protectors, I like to begin with a low psycholytic dose and allow the client's protector parts to feel some semblance of control as they transition into a more profound experience. Afterward, we allot adequate time to integrate all that happened and bring in the protectors and managers to witness and be updated on the psychedelic session.

Explaining Consent

Explicitly explain consent. Unfortunately, many clients, particularly those who have suffered abuse, have not learned this essential concept. Do not assume clients understand consent. I explain I will never touch them other than holding their hands if they request it or if they are in acute danger (e.g., falling off the couch or needing assistance to reach the restroom).

Explain that they are not passive receivers of psychedelic medicine but rather active participants collaborating with the drug and their healthcare team. We discuss and agree upon the dose. I let them know they can say *no* to receiving the medicine until they swallow the pill or receive the injection. Of course, once the medicine is taken, they are committed until it wears off. I also encourage them to address the medicine like it is a co-therapist and collaborator.

Trauma Mapping before the Medicine Session

It is crucial the therapist gets a sense of the client's trauma history before a psychedelic medicine session. Trauma mapping is a process of visualizing and understanding how trauma has affected an individual or even a community. This technique is used in therapy to help people explore their past experiences of trauma and how it has impacted their present lives, as well as educate the therapist about the client's history.

Trauma mapping can help people gain insight into their experiences of trauma, identify patterns and triggers, and develop strategies for coping and healing. The trauma-mapping technique I use most often is the EMDR Floatback Technique. Before using this method, clinicians must take at least Weekend I of EMDR training at the EMDR Institute.

For those trained in EMDR, here is the worksheet for the Floatback Technique.

EMDR Floatback Technique Worksheet

1. Current presenting issue or memory:
   "What incident or memory would you like to work on today?"
2. Image:
   "When you think about that memory, what image represents the worst part?"
3. Emotions:
   "When you bring up that picture/incident now, what emotions do you feel?"
4. Location of bodily sensation:
   "Where do you feel that in your body?"
5. Floatback:
   "I'd like you to bring up that picture, notice how it feels and where you feel it in your body, and let your mind trace when or how this first could have started."
   "Just feel and let it come to you."
   Ask, "What did you get?" If they say it goes back to a picture or a memory, ask for the image.
   If you decide to go back further, say, "Bring up that picture and let your mind trace back from there."
   Ask, "What do you get?"
   Do that until it returns to a "touchstone" (usually a childhood) memory.

This Floatback Technique is anchored in bodily sensations and developing awareness of when we are triggered and the patterns of bodily sensations, emotions, and negative beliefs that are bound together. This process illuminates how trauma is held in these matrices, and this awareness often helps clients observe and dismantle this entanglement in the psychedelic space. You can learn more about the Floatback Technique and other EMDR techniques by becoming trained in EMDR. Please refer to the Resources section for training programs.

Significant Life Events Timeline

Once I sense the client feels some safety, I begin to gently ask open-ended questions such as:
- How were emotions processed in the family you grew up in?
- What was it like growing up in your family?
- Tell me about elementary school/middle school/high school/college.

I create a timeline of important events that clients share, both positive and negative. Of course, there are often significant life events not mentioned, but it helps to get the gist of a person's general life trajectory and detect major patterns like attachment wounds and relational patterns. What is shared is just as significant as what is not shared that might emerge later. Being curious about how the client has made sense of their life events, or the inverse, their oblivion to repeated patterns of events, is an effective way to sense their self-perception and how they see themselves fitting or not fitting into the outside world.

Parts Mapping

While, from the beginning of a therapeutic relationship, IFS therapists listen for people's parts, proceeding from trauma mapping, therapists can begin a more formal process of "parts mapping." This technique involves helping the client identify and understand the different parts of themselves and explore how these parts interact. The therapist works with the client to explore the feelings, thoughts, and behaviors associated with other parts and understand how these parts might contribute to the client's current difficulties.

By understanding and working with these parts, the client can gain insight into their internal conflicts and emotional struggles and develop greater self-awareness and self-acceptance.

Firefighters, Rubberbanding, and Punisher Parts (Oh, My!)

Proceeding too quickly with psychedelic medicine and not spending adequate time obtaining consent from firefighters and protector parts can lead to the rubberband effect, punishment, and backlash after the session. I often hear therapists lament how their client did great in the psychedelic session, only to have a terrible relapse days after.

"Firefighters" take over during stress, crisis, or trauma to protect the person from feeling the pain of the underlying emotions. The "rubberbanding" parts keep a person stuck in a pattern of behavior, feeling, or belief by pulling them back to the past. The "punisher" parts are critical and self-punishing. They tend to hold self-blame and guilt; they believe they are responsible for the traumatic event and are punishing themselves for it. These parts are often identified and worked with in IFS therapy to help the individual understand and heal from past traumas and emotional difficulties. Understanding these different parts and their roles in the person's life can help clients create greater self-awareness and self-acceptance, leading to healing and change.

It is essential therapists explicitly contact the firefighter and protector parts immediately after the psychedelic session to make sure they understand what happened and check in with how they are feeling.

9

WORKING WITH THE PSYCHEDELIC

The PANTHER Method Continued

Fear

It is said that before entering the sea
a river trembles with fear.
She looks back at the path she has traveled,
from the peaks of the mountains,
the long winding road crossing forests and villages.
And in front of her,
she sees an ocean so vast,
that to enter
there seems nothing more than to disappear forever.
But there is no other way.
The river can not go back.
Nobody can go back.
To go back is impossible in existence.
The river needs to take the risk
of entering the ocean
because only then will fear disappear,
because that's where the river will know
it's not about disappearing into the ocean,
but of becoming the ocean.

—KHALIL GIBRAN

In the last chapter, we covered the preparation for the medicine journey and the P, A, N, and T (Preparation, Attunement, Needs of the protectors, and Trauma mapping) steps of psychedelic treatment. Each step is vital in laying the groundwork for the psychedelic journey. Taking time to adequately prepare sets the stage for the medicine day. In Chapter Nine, we discuss the steps H and E (Hold space and Empathy and engagement) steps, which take place during the medicine journey. Finally, in Chapter Ten we discuss the final stage of psychedelic therapy, the R (Resolution and integration) step.

Holding Space

This is H in the PANTHER acronym. What does it mean to "hold space" in a psychedelic journey? It's a term thrown around a great deal, but few people know how to do it well. Holding space is offering a sense of attunement, patience, and curiosity. In IFS terms, it is being in Self energy so that you can extend that energy to the journeyer. Self energy, in turn, is internalized into their system.

Clients arriving on medicine day are often nervous about a new experience. You, the therapist, must be on time, in your Self energy, and warmly welcome them into the space to help them feel settled. Remember how sacred it is to witness someone in such a vulnerable and intimate situation. I thank my guides for the honor of working with this client.

Allow adequate time to set up their "nest" of blankets and pillows and hold calm, patient energy. Ensure their headphones are charged, their phone is silenced, the playlist is ready, they have used the restroom, and their eyeshades are nearby. Check in about their ride home. Briefly catch up and revisit the intention they made in the preparation session. Do a brief body scan and ask if all the parts feel safe to proceed and consent to receive the medicine. If they say no, honor this with compassion and patience. Discuss the dose and ask if all their parts feel comfortable.

If you are licensed to provide psychedelic medicine, give the dose, or allow the medical provider to provide the medicine. Have the client wear the headphones and eyeshades, and offer them a blanket, as temperature shifts can occur.

Be sure the music playlist is curated for the duration and trajectory of the journey. If using a streaming platform, be sure there will not be advertisements playing and the music tracks are not in "shuffle" mode. I create customized invocations for each client based on their treatment plan. My clients seem to appreciate this special attention and care. My meditations/invocations last approximately ten to fifteen minutes as the medicine is metabolized. Guided meditations gently usher them into the psychedelic space and calm their nervous system. In the invocation, I remind them of their intention.

Holding space is also knowing when to intervene and give support and when to hang back and allow the client to work their own internal process. As mentioned before, Dr. Bill Richards taught me the acronym WAIT before talking to a client. This stands for "Why Am I Talking?" Ask yourself this before engaging with clients. Using WAIT is a way to scan your own parts and intentions. Ask yourself whether you are talking more to soothe yourself or for the client's well-being. I generally do not touch my clients during their sessions. Touch takes them out of their journeys and orients them toward the outside world. Of course, if they're frightened, I offer a hand to hold. But more effective than touch, I have found that moving into closer proximity to the client and slowly and quietly taking deep, nourishing breaths with long, slow exhalations is more beneficial than touch or words.

If your client does reach out for your hand, I recommend offering it immediately, as previously agreed in the preparation session. Be warm and emotionally available, but as soon as possible, retract your hand to allow them to return to their own space. Sometimes, a journeyer is processing material about abandonment or a lack of emotional availability of early caretakers, and offering a warm hand and calm presence is a corrective experience.

As discussed in previous sections, as facilitators, we show up in the therapeutic space with the totality of who we are and our work to become more self-aware. It is essential to have an understanding of our internal systems, countertransferences, and projections. Being grounded in Self energy allows the generosity of attunement.

Empathy and Engagement

This is E in the PANTHER acronym. Empathy and engagement are essential for a psychotherapist to connect and communicate effectively with clients. Empathy allows the therapist to understand and relate to the client's thoughts, feelings, and experiences, which can help to build trust and a sense of safety and rapport within the therapeutic relationship. By understanding and relating to the client's experiences, the therapist can help the client feel understood and validated, reducing feelings of isolation and alienation.

Engagement is the therapist's ability to actively participate in the therapy session and be present and fully attentive to the client. An engaged therapist can create a safe and supportive environment for clients to explore their thoughts and feelings. They provide feedback and guidance on the client's progress and can help set therapy goals and objectives. The therapist's engagement also helps the client feel heard and seen, fostering a sense of trust and safety within the therapeutic relationship. Engagement also means being fully present during the session. Even when the client has their mask on and they are deep in the journey, if you remain meditative and engaged, the client will sense this on some level.

10
RESOLUTION AND INTEGRATION

"Psychedelic experiences are notoriously difficult
to integrate into everyday life,
but it is precisely in this process
that their meaning becomes transformative."

—STAN GROF

Last, but far from least, is R in the PANTHER acronym: resolution and integration. Integration actually begins on medicine day as clients emerge and want to share their experiences. Sharing on medicine day is a good time to anchor the journey because the protector system is still downregulated. In the case of ketamine, it also helps clients remember their journeys. I call this special time The Golden Hour.

If possible, schedule an integration appointment the day after medicine day. If this is not possible, ask the client to send an email within twenty-four hours, sharing how they are feeling and what they remember. If an appointment the following day isn't an option, schedule the integration appointment as soon as possible. The processing often continues after the journey, so when you see them again, your client may be further along in this process than when they leave the office on medicine day.

The Golden Hour

After the medicine has been metabolized, and when the protector system is still asleep, I call this time "The Golden Hour." It is a potent time to

175

do some work with the exile system. Preintegration begins in the Golden Hour. It takes skill and experience to recognize when clients are ready to engage and speak. Some people spontaneously begin talking, and others may need a gentle nudge. Start by softly asking, "(Client name), what are you noticing?" If they cannot be coherent or track the question, this indicates they are still out of their body and normal mind. Allow them to journey for a while, and then ask again. If they begin talking, encourage them to keep the eye mask on and share what they experienced.

Help clients remember what they share by repeating their phrases. It helps if you take notes. Ask them to anchor three of their most salient experiences. These may be visual, auditory, emotional, or somatic. Sometimes, in the Golden Hour, we have time to explore presented symbols. Experienced psychedelic practitioners understand there are no bad trips. Whatever content arises, putting meaning to it and integration is what gives it relevance to the person's life. Help clients weave the content, symbols, and messages into their stories. As discussed in the first part of this book, creating meaning is essential.

Integration begins with the Golden Hour on medicine day. With the help of the therapist, clients can more easily proceed through the IFS unburdening step of releasing the burden to the elements of fire, earth, air, or water. I encourage somatic expressions of release: body movements, sighs, and emotion in releasing the burdens.

As the integration continues on the days following the experience, begin the session with a brief meditation to go inside, recall what it was like in the psychedelic space, and establish what parts are present and which ones the client wants to work with and get to know. Often, once people have had an experience with a psychedelic, they can more readily return to the experienced sense of connection and peace. Ask them what they are currently processing. You could ask questions like, "How have you changed?" and, "What new behaviors and thoughts are you noticing?"

Integration is important. If an additional integration session is needed, take the time to do this before returning to another psychedelic session.

When the content of the journeys has been properly metabolized and integrated, the client experiences a sense of relief. Once a resolution is found, the process has a sense of completion. The Hero's/Heroine's Journey is cyclical and never reaches a final destination. However, there can be closure once the presenting issue(s) the client initially sought treatment for is resolved, even if just for now. In the final therapy session, explore if there is a sense of peace and if they have reached a place to pause or conclude treatment. I always say that they can resume therapy if they need future support.

Using Archetypes with IFS during Integration

As mentioned in previous chapters, psychedelics are inherently archetypal. Archetypal psychology has renewed relevance after the journey and is fruitful for therapists to explore. These agents frequently produce vibrant symbols and archetypal content. I often wonder how much C.G. Jung and William James would have enjoyed facilitating psychedelic sessions and listening to all the fantastic tales of psychedelic journeys. I offer this here because sometimes, during psycholytic trips, clients talk about archetypal content and middose ketamine journeys as soon as they emerge from the experience. You can also discuss archetypes with your client in the integration sessions following the medicine session.

Many practitioners and psychedelic journeyers are perplexed by the content of their experiences. Facilitators should read the works of C.G. Jung and Joseph Campbell to understand how they might work with this material. The Theradelic Approach pays close attention to symbolic content and is curious about how it relates to the internal family system. Begin by asking the client to recall as much of their journey as possible as they emerge from the experience. Ask for the main content of what they saw, heard, sensed, and felt. Record any symbolic content they offer and the emotion attached to it, then ask the journeyer what the symbol might mean to them. Allow them to engage with curiosity. Avoid directing or telling them how it relates to their life. Enjoy the process of discovery. Of course, if a client doesn't feel like talking after the experience, do not press them. Remain attuned and track their needs.

When the content is shared, work with the Six Fs in IFS:
– Find
– Focus
– Feel toward
– beFriend
– Flesh out
– Fears and concerns

This process will help you work with the parts that sent the symbol to the journeyer. Use In-Sight or direct access to ask the part or parts related to the symbol what they are trying to communicate to your client. It is important to note each person has a specific relationship to archetypal content. There isn't a universal symbol for "mother," "sun," or "snake." I avoid using dream symbol directories that dictate what the symbol means. The meaning is internal. A story of how I use IFS and Jungian symbol analysis follows.

Case Story

As a client emerged from a middose ketamine journey, she reported experiencing herself as a "beetle fairy." She shared this in a soft voice with reverence and awe. She felt carefree and was flying among the green plants and wildflowers in a field. The first part of the experience was lovely. Suddenly, she realized her wings were becoming sticky. She had difficulty flying and found herself tumbling to Earth and landing on a plant leaf. She was horrified to find her wings had become glued onto her back. No matter how much she tried to get them loose, they remained stuck. She struggled like this for what seemed like a very long time. After crying out, two female fairy beetles came to her. She was initially afraid they would attack, but instead, they worked together, one on each side, peeling the wings up and off her back. The process was prolonged and painful. She said she was curled up in the yogic Child's Pose as they worked to loosen her wings. They were wet like a healed broken arm just after the cast is removed. She opened her wings and dried them in the sunshine. The sun's warmth felt terrific. Her journey content continued with chapters of visuals and symbols, but this section of the experience was the most salient.

Often, I have heard therapists respond to trip reports by laughing dismissively about unusual visual hallucinations. "Oh, weird! The crazy stuff we see on trips!" If I had done so, my client would have felt shame for sharing this experience. It is also a missed opportunity to react in this way. Therapists must check in with their own parts that dismiss trip stories and become aware of parts that block openness and curiosity about the material.

During the integration, my client initially laughed at the strangeness of being a fairy beetle with sticky wings, but I pressed her to explore the content. Her defensive parts were coming back online.

"What do you think that means to you, being a beetle fairy?" I asked. She was still in the Golden Hour, and her managers sensed all was well and went back to sleep. She answered in a childlike voice, "I feel free in the sunshine. Like I can play." I noted the childlike voice and the response in the present tense. "Are you there now?" Childlike nod. I sat back and left her to explore for a few minutes peacefully. After about ten minutes, she softly said, "Am I back?" I asked, "(Her name), what are you noticing now?" She said, "I was so happy there," but now she said it wistfully.

I noted the past tense and the shift in emotion. I proceeded to begin the unblending process. At that point, we had contracted with a protector part that felt like betrayal is inevitable with other women. Once unblended, I asked, "I'm curious about the beetle fairy and what happened to her wings and the other beetle fairies who came to help. Why did you show (client name) that?" The inquiry opened up a fascinating story about how the protector part wanted her to understand how she has trust issues with women. Her mother was emotionally neglectful and critical. She would send mixed messages of being helpful but then turn on my client as a child and punish her daughter's vulnerability.

Once unburdened, the lesson the part wanted to communicate was that sometimes we need help from others, and we must take the risk of surrendering to receive support; that not all women are dangerous, and she could trust people who behave in trustworthy ways. I asked her if anything was happening in her current life that reminded her of that lesson. She was delighted to put the puzzle together. Two women in her office had recently tried to befriend her by inviting her to lunch, but she had made excuses because she wasn't sure of their intentions. She realized she had transferred her mistrust of her mother's intentions onto adult friendships with other women. The Self-led part was trying to encourage her to give women a chance to prove they are trustworthy.

Closing Appointments

Repeat as many sessions as are necessary for your client. I repeat the PANTHER steps as many times as required. I generally space the ketamine appointments one to two weeks apart, but the finances and schedules of my clients, and my own schedule, can influence the cadence. I usually recommend three to six KAP sessions and a reassessment, and I work closely with my medical provider colleague and team.

When the patient and I have addressed their mental health concerns, we discuss whether they want to continue regular hourly therapy or space out the ketamine therapy sessions. When we decide to conclude our time together, we schedule a closing session. I like to recap their growth and what changes they have noticed. I give an overview of the development I have witnessed in them. I remind them of the Eight Cs of Self-leadership and our conversation at the beginning about which C they are calling more of into their life. I ask if this has been addressed and how they feel about that energy they wanted to work on. We discuss the next few months' self-care goals. I let my clients know my door is always open.

11

SELF-CARE, GROUP SESSIONS, AND PSYCHOLYTIC DOSING

The Importance of Self-Care

We are only with our clients for one to three hours a week. That leaves a lot of time between sessions. Daily self-care can supplement therapy in positive ways. Self-care is essential to overall well-being and is crucial for people undergoing psychotherapy. Regular self-care practices support the therapeutic process by providing balance and stability and fostering a sense of self-compassion and self-awareness. Directly spending time in therapy sessions understanding a client's self-care regimen and educating if you notice a lack of self-care can maximize the effectiveness of therapy.

Exercise, meditation, and spiritual practices are productive ways to promote self-care. Exercise has been shown to impact physical and mental health positively and can effectively relieve stress. Meditation and spiritual practices can help reduce stress and anxiety and provide inner peace and connection. Research has shown that regular meditation practice can improve cognitive function and emotional regulation and reduce symptoms of depression and anxiety (Goyal et al. 2014). Volunteering, helping others and the environment, caring for animals and nature, and expressing gratitude can also contribute to self-care. They can promote feelings of connectedness and purpose and improve overall well-being (Emmons and McCullough, 2003).

Another important aspect of self-care is getting adequate sleep and nutrition. These critical aspects affect how we perceive and assimilate information. They greatly influence our thoughts, feelings, and ability to be resilient and meet life's challenges. Sufficient sleep is essential for overall physical and mental health and can help to improve mood, cognitive function, and stress management. A healthy diet that includes nutrient-dense foods can also provide essential nutrients and energy to support physical and mental well-being.

Another crucial aspect of self-care is belonging to a community, which can give a sense of purpose, support, and connection. Studies have shown that social support can improve overall well-being, reduce stress, and promote mental health (House, Landis, and Umberson 1988). A client's social network is significant with regard to the integration of psychedelic journeys. Psychedelic experiences are frequently life-changing, and having a circle of loved ones who can help the client absorb, understand, and assimilate journey insights into daily life can be incredibly helpful. Many clients do not have a support system; in this case, refer them to a psychedelic integration group.

Group Psychedelic Sessions

One of my favorite ways to work with psychedelic medicine is in a group setting. In addition to the medicine session, therapists can conduct preparation and integration in group sessions. Medicine-day sessions in groups create an enriching way to process experiences together. I enjoy integrating IFS therapy after a group middose ketamine experience. There is some magic and alchemy in the group process, particularly if the facilitator is adept at creating safety in the group container. As one person offers a vulnerable exile to be unburdened, another person's exile will inevitably be vicariously processed simultaneously. An extra dimension of the unburdening of extreme parts occurs when a "tribe" of sympathetic people witnesses someone working with their IFS practitioner. The group can validate and assure the journeyer of their inherent goodness and well-being. Parts in others heal parts of ourselves.

In all group experiences, it is essential to discuss confidentiality beforehand. What is shared in the group stays in the group. We only discuss people and their processes within the group experience. I confirm that everyone agrees to abide by confidentiality in every group, and I screen participants carefully to create group cohesiveness. I have a saying that, for the group experience, I screen for "high vibe and low drama." The group can only go as far or as deep as the lowest-functioning member. Be aware of bringing people together within a similar functioning and mental health bandwidth. Doing so creates a better experience for everyone.

I work with higher-needs clients individually before inviting them to join a group experience. It isn't fair to throw people with attachment challenges or social anxiety into a group experience and not be able to give them the individual attention they require. Once they have completed a few individual ketamine sessions and feel ready to join a larger cohort, they are welcomed into the group experience. I had a client I saw for many years with an adverse childhood experience (ACE) score of nine out of ten. He had such disorganized attachment and trauma that he had difficulty regulating his anxiety in groups. It would have been unfair to put him in a group ketamine experience before he was ready. We worked in individual therapy and several KAP sessions for a year. He had several profound breakthroughs around social awkwardness and anxiety. He began reporting he was maintaining friendships and asked to attend a group session. He had a wonderful experience in the group retreat and added much to the richness of the group process. This hybrid way of working individually and in groups can benefit many clients.

Psycholytic Dosages

"Psycholytic" refers to a type of psychotherapy involving low to moderate doses of psychedelic substances in combination with talk therapy, EMDR, IFS, somatic, or other therapy modalities. This approach aims to use the psychedelic experience to help clients gain insight into their unconscious thoughts, feelings, and behaviors and to work through psychological issues such as trauma, anxiety, and depression. Psycholytic therapy differs from traditional psychedelic therapy, which relies on higher doses and tends to focus on deeper psychological, spiritual, and transcendental experiences.

I use psycholytic doses frequently for both individual and group ketamine therapy sessions. It dovetails beautifully with IFS because the protectors are quieted, and there is more direct access to exiled parts. I also frequently use EMDR phases three through eight during a psycholytic-dose ketamine session.

Clients can often speak throughout the session and remain in a light trance. Psycholytic sessions tend to last two to three hours, and a much lighter dose of ketamine is used. These methods require specific training to perform them safely and effectively. Psychedelics, especially ketamine, are "heart-opening" in small doses and soften the defense system. Therapists spend a lot of time and energy helping clients open into deeper processing. Psycholytic doses can facilitate this and give access to hidden exiles that are normally difficult to reach due to protectors. Because of the ease of accessing exiles during a psychedelic session, it is essential to receive permission from protectors before proceeding further into the session. Additionally, the therapist must update the protectors as part of the integration session. Protectors must be explicitly informed about what occurred during the previous session while the medicine sent them "off duty." This step profoundly reduces backlash and punishment and helps exiles stay free and unburdened.

Case Study: When Low Doses Are More Effective

A client sought therapy with a presenting issue of feeling like life didn't matter and had no meaning. He wasn't actively suicidal and didn't have suicidal ideations. He had a flat affect and a monotone voice. He was married to a woman he went to high school with, and they grew up in the same small town. They met at church. His father was a policeman, and he also served in law enforcement. My client was also a police officer like his father. He had experienced a few terrible things as a police officer, but the worst was the injustice he observed in society against disadvantaged people. He had been in the military and suffered from PTSD. He would have episodes of paranoia triggered by fireworks on the Fourth of July or when people crowded him in public spaces. As a child, he recalled his father as being overbearing, abusive, and an alcoholic. This client felt intense anger towards his mother because, in his view, she enabled his father by being passive. He resented her not taking him and his two sisters away from their father's harmful ways.

This client had been prescribed high-dose ketamine lozenges by a company that mailed ketamine to people for use at home. The medicine was not accompanied by psychotherapy except for a brief call every few weeks. He would take the lozenges, dissociate for a few hours, and feel mild relief from his PTSD symptoms. However, the relief was fleeting and didn't last longer than two or three days. Then he would feel flat and empty again. He came to see me for psychotherapy, and we started a treatment protocol for IFS and EDMR.

After a few sessions, he asked if we could start ketamine sessions. I agreed, but I suggested doing psycholytic dose sessions and continuing our IFS work while he was on a low dose of intramuscularly injected ketamine. He was perplexed by this proposal, as he was used to much higher doses. "I can handle a really big dose," he said. I assured him that I didn't doubt he could handle it, but I felt he was using the medicine to dissociate rather than work on deeper issues that caused the distress. After processing during a subsequent preparation session, we agreed he was ready for the psycholytic session.

In the preparation session, I took him through the meditation, asking to get consent from his protectors and whether they had any questions or concerns. They were quiet, and we proceeded to the psycholytic session.

The healthcare provider gave him a twenty-milligram intramuscular injection during the session, and we began the IFS process. Fairly quickly, he saw himself standing in a field behind his childhood home as a young part of his internal ecosystem. This part was an effeminate young boy who liked to wear dresses and play with dolls. As we explored and worked with this part, it showed him how terrified he was of his dad. His father would threaten to beat him if he acted "like a f***ing sissy." The memory was distressing, and we worked to care for and unburden the exile using the steps in IFS. Once we got to the "feel toward" step, and he felt compassion toward the exile, he got the internalized judging parts to step out and give us some space. We proceeded through the unburdening process. He was able to come to a place of compassion for this sensitive part of him. He recognized he has a tender, feminine part that was shunned and ridiculed by his father. The abuse was so incredibly painful that he internalized it as an exile, creating hypercritical and overcompensating masculine protectors to cover up the exile so no one could see it. The dissociated parts kept him numb whenever he ventured close to the exile he was terrified to discover.

It is impressive, with the help of low-dose ketamine, how quickly we can work with tender exiles. However, this always alerts me to be particularly cautious about updating protectors to prevent backlash when we wrap up the session. As he emerged from the session, I asked if his protectors saw everything that had happened. We updated the protectors about the unburdening. At this point he realized that the dissociation he had experienced, both in his regular life and during the high-dose ketamine lozenge sessions, were ways his protectors blocked him from getting to know the sensitive exile. It had felt too dangerous to reveal that part. In the subsequent integration sessions, we worked with his parts to keep the sensitive, young parts of him safe from ridicule. We continued our psycholytic and integration sessions. Over time, he was able to express himself better. His voice was no longer flat, and he felt relief from depression. His marriage also improved, as his wife was relieved to have access to compassionate and calm energy from his Self.

CONCLUSION

Thank you for exploring the fantastic world of psychedelic-assisted therapy using the Theradelic Approach. The Theradelic Approach is an orientation toward how to be an effective, compassionate, and ethical psychedelic-assisted psychotherapist. Using the PANTHER method creates a structure for the therapy process within the model.

I hope this book has offered a broader perspective of what it means to become a great psychedelic therapist. You may use the Theradelic Approach to help a broad spectrum of clientele with many different needs. Incorporating effective therapeutic modalities into your psychedelic therapy practice increases your treatment's effectiveness and extends the duration of the medicine's positive effects.

More well-trained therapists are in demand as psychedelic medicine becomes more ubiquitous and available. We need hundreds of thousands of well-trained psychedelic practitioners to meet the needs of a society suffering from trauma, depression, and anxiety. I hope this book has inspired you to explore methodologies such as IFS, EMDR, and archetypal psychology to diversify your tool kit and add depth and creativity to your practice.

Each healthcare practitioner has their own "special medicine" they can offer clients. Your special medicine is your specific licensure, training, and skill set, along with how and who you are in the world. Your unique medicine is your integrity combined with how you hold space, care for your clients, and attune to them. Add your special magic to the Theradelic Approach formula. Self-lead with the Eight Cs, and find ways to be more creative, connected, compassionate, and confident in your ability to hold space and offer excellent preparation and integration of psychedelic journeys.

The citizens of Earth are facing existential crises, the likes of which we have never known. Our world needs these medicines and their healing potential more than ever.

BIBLIOGRAPHY

Agin-Liebes, Gabrielle, Trevor F. Haas, Rafael Lancelotta, Malin V. Uthaug, Johannes G. Ramaekers, and Alan K. Davis. 2021. *ACS Pharmacology & Translational Science*, 4 (2): 543–552. https://doi.org/10.1021/acsptsci.1c00018.

Amorim, João. A., Giuseppe Coppotelli, Anabela P. Rolo, Carlos M. Palmeira, Jaime M. Ross, and David A. Sinclair. 2022. "Mitochondrial and metabolic dysfunction in ageing and age-related diseases." *Nature Reviews Endocrinology* 18: 243–258. https://doi.org/10.1038/s41574-021-00626-7.

Anderson, G. T. and H. H. Maurer. 2018. "Mescaline: A review of the pharmacology and therapeutic potential of peyote's principal alkaloid." *Journal of Psychopharmacology*, 32 (4): 393–404.

Anderson, L.D. and M. Polanco. 2019. "Psychedelics, trauma, and mental health: A review of the clinical and preclinical evidence." *Journal of Psychoactive Drugs*, 51 (1): 1–9.

Andrews-Hanna, Jessica R., Jay S. Reidler, Christine Huang, and Randy L. Buckner. 2010. "Evidence for the default network's role in spontaneous cognition." *Journal of Neurophysiology*, 104 (1): 322–35. https://doi.org/10.1152/jn.00830.2009.

Bacon, Francis. 1620. *Novum Organum*. London: John Bill.

Bacon, Francis. 1884. *The Works of Francis Bacon, Volume 1, Essays*, edited by Basil Montegu. New York: R. Worthington.

Baldwin, S. A., B. Anderson, and F. G. Lu. 2011. "Internal Family Systems Therapy as a treatment for veterans with posttraumatic stress disorder." *Journal of Clinical Psychology*, 67 (3): 221–231.

Barrett, Frederick S., Manoj K. Doss, Nathan D. Sepeda, James J. Pekar, and Roland R. Griffiths. 2020. "Emotions and Brain Function Are Altered up to One Month After a Single High Dose of Psilocybin." *Scientific Reports – Nature*, 10: 2214. https://doi.org/10.1038/s41598-020-59282-y.

Blake, William. 1868. *The Marriage of Heaven and Hell: In Full Color*. London: Camden Hotten.

Boyle, Gregory. 2021. *Review of the Whole Language: The Power of Extravagant Tenderness*. Maryland: Avid Reader Press.

Bremner, J. Douglas. 2002. *Does Stress Damage the Brain? Understanding Trauma-Related Disorders from a Mind-Body Perspective*. New York: W. W. Norton & Company.

Brown, Daniel P., and David S. Elliott. 2016. *Attachment Disturbances in Adults: Treatment for Comprehensive Repair*. New York: W. W. Norton & Company.

Campbell, Joseph. 1991. *A Joseph Campbell Companion: Reflections on the Art of Living*, edited by Diane K. Osbon. New York: Harper Perennial.

Campbell, Joseph. (1949) 1993. *The Hero With a Thousand Faces*. Reprint, London: Fontana Press.

Campbell, Joseph. 2004. *Pathways to Bliss: Mythology and Personal Transformation*. Novato: New World Library.

Carhart-Harris, Robin L., Mark Bolstridge, James Rucker, Camilla M. J. Day, David Erritzoe, Mendel Kaelen, Michael Bloomfield et al. 2016. "Psilocybin with psychological support for treatment-resistant depression: An open-label feasibility study." *The Lancet Psychiatry*, 3, no. 7 (July): 619–627. https://doi.org/10.1016/S2215-0366(16)30065-7.

Carhart-Harris, Robin, Bruna Giribaldi, Rosalind Watts, Michelle Baker-Jones, Ashleigh Murphy-Beiner, Roberta Murphy, Jonny Martell, Allan Blemings, David Erritzoe, and David J. Nutt. 2021. "Trial of Psilocybin Versus Escitalopram for Depression." *The New England Journal of Medicine*, 384: 1402–1411. https://doi.org/10.1056/NEJMoa2032994.

Cassidy, Jude and Phillip R. Shaver. 1999. "Handbook of Attachment: Theory, Research, and Clinical Applications, Second Edition." *Journal of the Canadian Academy of Child and Adolescent Psychiatry*, 19, (1) (February) :57–58.

Castelnuovo, Gianluca, Isabel Fernandez, and Benedikt L. Amann. 2019. "Editorial: Present and Future of EMDR in Clinical Psychology and Psychotherapy." *Frontiers in Psychology*, 10. https://doi.org/10.3389/fpsyg.2019.02185.

Center for Nonviolent Communication website. n.d. "What is NVC?" Accessed April 11, 2023. https://www.cnvc.org/learn-nvc/what-is-nvc.

Chödrön, Pema. 1996. *When Things Fall Apart: Heart Advice for Difficult Times*. Boston: Shambhala.

Copper Canyon Press. (2013). Border of a Dream: Selected Poems (p. 281).

Davis, Alan K., Sara So, Rafael Lancelotta, Joseph P. Barsuglia, and Roland R. Griffiths. 2019. "5-methoxy-*N,N*-dimethyltryptamine (5-MeO-DMT) used in a naturalistic group setting is associated with unintended improvements in depression and anxiety." *The American Journal of Drug and Alcohol Abuse*, 45, (2) (March): 161–169. https://doi.org/10.1080/00952990.2018.1545024.

Davoodvandi, Maryam, Shokouh Navabi Nejad, and Valiollah Farzad. 2021. "Examining the Effectiveness of Gottman Couple Therapy on Improving Marital Adjustment and Couples' Intimacy." *Iranian Journal of Psychiatry*, 13 (2): 135–141.

Daws, Richard E., Christopher Timmermann, Bruna Giribaldi, James D. Sexton, Matthew B. Wall, David Erritzoe, Leor Roseman, David Nutt, and Robin Carhart-Harris. 2022. "Increased global integration in the brain after psilocybin therapy for depression." *Nature Medicine*, 28: 844–851. https://doi.org/10.1038/s41591-022-01744-z.

DEA website. n.d. "Drug Scheduling." Accessed March 21, 2023. https://www.dea.gov/drug-information/drug-scheduling.

Emmons, Robert. A. and Michael E. McCullough. 2003. "Counting Blessings Versus Burdens: An Experimental Investigation of Gratitude and Subjective Well-Being in Daily Life." *Journal of Personality and Social Psychology*, 84 (2): 377–389. https://doi.org/10.1037/0022-3514.84.2.377.

Fava, Maurizio, Marlene P. Freeman, Martina Flynn, Heidi Judge, Bettina B Hoeppner, Cristina Cusin, Dawn F. Ionescu et. al. 2018. "Double-blind, placebo-controlled, dose-ranging trial of intravenous ketamine as adjunctive therapy in treatment-resistant depression (TRD)." *Molecular Psychiatry*, 25 (7): 1592–1603. https://doi.org/10.1038/s41380-018-0256-5.

Fehr, Ernst and Urs Fischbacher. 2004. "Third-Party Punishment and Social Norms." *Evolution and Human Behavior*, 25 (2) (March): 63–87. https://doi.org/10.1016/S1090-5138(04)00005-4.

Fonagy, P, G. Gergely, E. L. Jurist, and M. Target. 2002. *Affect Regulation, Mentalization, and the Development of the Self*. New York: Other Press.

Freud, Sigmund and Josef Breuer. 1895. *Studies on Hysteria*. Translated by James Strachey. London: Hogarth Press.

Fuentes, Juan José, Francina Fonseca, Matilde Elices, Magí Farré, and Marta Torrens. 2019. "Therapeutic Use of LSD in Psychiatry: A Systematic Review of Randomized-Controlled Clinical Trials." *Frontiers in Psychiatry*, 10: 943. https://doi.org/10.3389/fpsyt.2019.00943.

Fuertes, Jairo. N., Charles J. Gelso, Jesse J. Owen, David Cheng. 2013. "Real Relationship, Working Alliance, Transference/Countertransference and Outcome in Time-Limited Counseling and Psychotherapy." *Counselling Psychology Quarterly*, 26 (3). https://doi.org/1 0.1080/09515070.2013.845548.

Gintis, Herbert, Samuel Bowles, Robert Boyd, and Ernst Fehr. 2003. "Explaining Altruistic Behavior in Humans." *Evolution and Human Behavior*, 24 (3): 153–172. https://doi. org/10.1016/S1090-5138(02)00157-5

Goyal, Madhav, Sonal Singh, Erica M. S. Sibinga, Neda F. Gould, Anastasia Rowland-Seymour, Ritu Sharma, Zackary Berger et al. 2014. "Meditation Programs for Psychological Stress and Well-Being." *JAMA Internal Medicine*, 174 (3): 357–368. https://doi.org/10.1001/ jamainternmed.2013.13018.

Greicius, M. D., B. Krasnow, A. L. Reiss, and V. Menon. 2004. "Default mode network activity and connectivity in major depressive disorder." *Biological Psychiatry*, 56 (3): 301–307.

Griffiths, R. R., W. A. Richards, U. McCann, and R. Jesse. 2006. "Psilocybin Can Occasion Mystical-Type Experiences Having Substantial and Sustained Personal Meaning and Spiritual Significance." *Psychopharmacology*, 187 (3): 268–82. https://doi.org/10.1007/ s00213-006-0457-5.

Griffiths, Roland R., Matthew W Johnson, Michael A Carducci, Annie Umbricht, William A. Richards, Brian D. Richards, Mary P. Cosimano, and Margaret A. Klinedinst. 2016. "Psilocybin produces substantial and sustained decreases in depression and anxiety in patients with life-threatening cancer: A randomized double-blind trial." *Journal of Psychopharmacology*, 30 (12): 1181–1197. https://doi. org/10.1177/0269881116675513.

Grof, Stanislav. 1985. *Beyond the Brain: Birth, Death, and Transcendence in Psychotherapy*. New York: State University of New York Press.

Grof, Stanislav. and Christina Grof. 1990. *The Stormy Search for the Self: A Guide to Personal Growth Through Transformational Crisis*. Los Angeles: J.P. Tarcher.

Grof, Christina and Stanislav. 2008. *Holotropic Breathwork: A New Approach to Self-Exploration and Therapy*. Rochester, Vermont: Inner Tradition – Bear & Company.

Grof, S. (2009). *LSD: Doorway to the numinous: The groundbreaking psychedelic research into realms of the human unconscious*. Park Street Press.

Halpern, J. H., A. R. Sherwood, J. I. Hudson, D. Yurgelun-Todd, and H. G. Pope. 2005. "Psychological and Cognitive Effects of Long-Term Peyote Use Among Native Americans." *Biological Psychiatry*, 60 (8), 624–631.

Harari, Yuval Noah. 2015. *Sapiens: A Brief History of Humankind*. New York: Harper.

Hart, Carl L. 2021. *Drug Use For Grown-Ups: Chasing Liberty In The Land Of Fear*. New York: Penguin Press.

Hillman, James. 1960. *Emotion: A Comprehensive Phenomenology of Theories and Their Meaning for Therapy*. Evanston, Illinois: Northwestern University Press.

Hillman, James. 1975. *Revisioning Psychology*. New York: Harper & Row.

Hillman, James. 1996. *The Soul's Code: In Search of Character and Calling*. Milsons Point, New South Wales: Random House Australia.

Hofmann Albert. 1979. *LSD, My Problem Child*. New York: McGraw-Hill.

Hollis, James. 2000. *The Archetypal Imagination*, 83. College Station: Texas A&M University Press.

House, J. S., K. R. Landis, and D. Umberson. 1988. "Social relationships and health." *Science*, 241 (4865): 540–5. https://doi.org/10.1126/science.3399889.

Jhang, Jia-Fong, Yung-Hsiang Hsu, Yuan-Hong Jiang, and Hann-Chorng Kuo. 2014. "Elevated Serum IdE May Be Associated with Development of Ketamine Cystitis." *The Journal of Urology*, 192 (4): 1249–1256. https://doi.org/10.1016/j.juro.2014.05.084.

Johnson, Matthew. W., Albert Garcia-Romeu, Mary P. Cosimano, and Roland R. Griffiths. 2014. "Pilot study of the 5-HT2AR agonist psilocybin in the treatment of tobacco addiction." *Journal of Psychopharmacology*, 28 (11): 983–992. https://doi.org/10.1177/0269881114548296.

Johnson, M. W., A. Garcia-Romeu, M. P. Cosimano, and R. R. Griffiths. 2017. "Psilocybin-assisted treatment for opioid addiction: A proof-of-concept study." *Journal of Psychoactive Drugs*, 49 (1): 1–10.

Johnson, Matthew W., Katherine A. MacLean, Chad J. Reissig, Thomas E. Prisinzano, and Roland R. Griffiths. 2011. "Human psychopharmacology and dose-effects of salvinorin A, a kappa opioid agonist hallucinogen present in the plant Salvia divinorum." *Drug and Alcohol Dependence*, 115 (1–2): 150–155. https://doi.org/10.1016/j.drugalcdep.2010.11.005.

Johnson, M. W., Richards, W. A., R. R. Griffiths, and B. D. Richards. 2008. "Human hallucinogen research: Guidelines for safety." *Journal of Psychopharmacology*, 22 (6): 603–620. https://doi.org/10.1177/0269881108093587.

Jung, Carl G. 1939. *The Integration of the Personality*. New York: Farrar & Rinehart.

Jung, Carl G. 1957. *The Undiscovered Self*. Princeton University Press.

Jung, Carl G. 1973. *Letters, Vol. 1*. Edited by Gerhard Adler. New York: Routledge.

Khalsa, S. S. and J. M. Greiner-Ferris. 2021. "Internal Family Systems Therapy for PTSD: A Randomized Controlled Trial." *Journal of Traumatic Stress*. 34 (1): 132–142. https://doi.org/10.1002/jts.22598.

Kouda Katsuyasu, Masayuki Iki. 2010. "Beneficial Effects of Mild Stress (Hormetic Effects): Dietary Restriction and Health." *Journal of Physiological Anthropology*, 29 (4): 127–32. https://doi.org/10.2114/jpa2.29.127.

Krystal, John H., Chadi G. Abdallah, Gerard Sanacora, Dennis S. Charney, and Ronald S. Duman. 2019. "Ketamine: A Paradigm Shift for Depression Research and Treatment." *Neuron*, 101 (5): 774–778. https://doi.org/10.1016/j.neuron.2019.02.005.

Kurtzman, Laura. 2022. "Psilocybin Rewires the Brain for People with Depression." University of California San Francisco. Accessed March 21, 2023. https://www.ucsf.edu/news/2022/04/422606/psilocybin-rewires-brain-people-depression.

Levenson, Hanna. 1981. "Differentiating Among Internality, Powerful Others, and Chance." In *Locus of Control: Current Trends in Theory and Research*, edited by H. M. Lefcourt, 15–49. Cambridge, MA: Academic Press.

Luoma, Jason B., Christina Chwyl, Geoff J. Bathje, Alan K. Davis, and Rafael Lancelotta. 2020. "A Meta-Analysis of Placebo-Controlled Trials of Psychedelic-Assisted Therapy." *Journal of Psychoactive Drugs*, 52 (4): 289–299. https://doi.org/10.1080/02791072.2020.1769878.

Mithoefer, Michael C. 2015. *A Manual for MDMA-Assisted Psychotherapy in the Treatment of Posttraumatic Stress Disorder*, Version 7 (August 19, 2015). Santa Cruz: Multidisciplinary Association for Psychedelic Studies (MAPS).

MacLean, Katherine A. Matthew W. Johnson, and Roland R. Griffiths. 2011. "Mystical Experiences Occasioned by the Hallucinogen Psilocybin Lead to Increases in the Personality Domain of Openness." *Journal of Psychopharmacology*, 25 (11): 1453–1461.

Machado, Antonio. 2003. *Border of a Dream: Selected Poems*. Port Townsend, WA: Copper Canyon Press.

Maté, Gabor and Daniel Maté. 2022. *The Myth of Normal: Trauma, Illness and Healing in a Toxic Culture*. Avery: New York.

Maté, Gabor. 2018. *In the Realm of Hungry Ghosts: Close Encounters with Addiction*. London: Vermilion.

McKenna, Terence. 1992. *Food of the Gods: The Search for the Original Tree of Knowledge*. London: Bantam.

Moreno, Francisco A., Christopher B. Wiegand, E. Keolani Taitano, and Pedro L. Delgado. 2006. "Safety, tolerability, and efficacy of psilocybin in 9 patients with obsessive-compulsive disorder." *Journal of Clinical Psychiatry*, 67(11), 1735–40. https://doi.org/10.4088/jcp.v67n1110.

Murdock, Maureen. 1990. *The Heroine's Journey: Woman's Quest for Wholeness*. Boston: Shambhala.

Nietzsche, Friedrich. 1883. *Thus Spoke Zarathustra: A Book for All and None*. Chemnitz: Ernst Schmeitzner.

Krebs, Teri S. and Pål-Ørjan Johansen. 2013. "Psychedelics and Mental Health: A Population Study." *PLoS One*, 8(8): e63972. https://doi.org/10.1371/journal.pone.0063972.

Nin, Anaïs. 1966. *The Diary of Anaïs Nin: Vol. I: 1931–1934*. New York: Swallow Press/ Harcourt, Brace & World.

Norcross, John C., Paul M. Krebs, and James O. Prochaska. 2010. "Stages of Change." *Journal of Clinical Psychology*, 67 (2): 143–154. https://doi.org/10.1002/jclp.20758.

Orner, Eva, director. *Bikram: Yogi, Guru, Predator*. Pulse Films, 2019. 1 hr., 26 min.

Osmond, Humphry. 1957. "A Review of the Clinical Effects of Psychotomimetic Agents." *Annals of the New York Academy of Sciences*: Vol. 66 (3): 418–434. https://doi.org/10.1111/j.1749-6632.1957.tb40738.x.

Osório, Flávia de L., Rafael F. Sanches, Ligia R. Macedo, Rafael G. dos Santos, João P. Maia-de-Oliveira, Lauro Wichert-Ana, Draulio B. de Araujo, Jordi Riba, José A. Crippa, Jaime E. Hallak. 2015. "Antidepressant Effects of a Single Dose of Ayahuasca in Patients with Recurrent Depression: A Preliminary Report." *Revista Brasileira de Psiquiatria*, 37 (3): 13–20. https://doi.org/10.1590/1516-4446-2014-1496.

Overmier, J. B. and M. E. Seligman. 1967. "Effects of Inescapable Shock Upon Subsequent Escape and Avoidance Responding." *Journal of Comparative and Physiological Psychology*, 63 (1): 28–33. https://doi.org/10.1037/h0024166.

Pahnke, W. N., A. A. Kurland, L. E. Goodman, and W. A. Richards. 1969. "LSD-Assisted Psychotherapy with Terminal Cancer Patients." *Current Psychiatric Therapies*, 9: 144–52.

Palhano-Fontes, Fernanda, Dayanna Barreto, Heloisa Onias, Katia C. Andrade, Morgana M. Novaes, Jessica A. Pessoa, Sergio A. Mota-Rolim et al. 2019. "Rapid Antidepressant Effects of the Psychedelic Ayahuasca in Treatment-Resistant Depression: A Randomized Placebo-Controlled Trial." *Psychological Medicine*, 49 (4): 655–663. https://doi.org/10.1017/S0033291718001356.

Pollan, Michael. 2018. *How to Change Your Mind: The New Science of Psychedelics*. London: Allen Lane.

Poole Heller, Diane. 2015. "Avoidant: Kind Eyes Exercise." Accessed March 21, 2023. https://dianepooleheller.com/avoidant-kind-eyes-exercise/.

Poole Heller, Diane. 2017. *Healing Your Attachment Wounds: How to Create Deep and Lasting Intimate Relationships*. Louisville: Sounds True Publishing.

Price, C. J., B. McBride, L. Hyerle, and D. M. Kivlighan. 2018. "Internal Family Systems Therapy as an Attachment-Based Intervention: Case Reports of Symptom Reduction in Trauma Clients." *Journal of Counseling & Development*, 96 (2): 155–164. https://doi.org/10.1002/jcad.12203.

Richards, William A. 2016. "Psychedelic Psychotherapy: Insights From 25 Years of Research." *Journal of Humanistic Psychology*, 57 (4): 323–337. https://doi.org/10.1177/0022167816670996.

Richards, William. A. 2015. *Sacred Knowledge: "Psychedelics and Religious Experience*. New York: Columbia University Press.

Richards, B. A. 2019. "Psilocybin, psychological well-being, and public policy." *International Journal of Drug Policy*, 69: 53–58.

Rothbaum, B. O. (2005). What Works for Whom? A Critical Review of Treatments for Posttraumatic Stress Disorder. In S. Taylor (Ed.), Clinician's Guide to Evidence-Based Practices: Mental Health and the Addictions (pp. 227-252). John Wiley & Sons.

Romeo, Bruno, Laurent Karila, Catherine Martelli, and Amine Benjamina. 2020. "Efficacy of Psychedelic Treatments on Depressive Symptoms: A Meta-Analysis." *Journal of Psychopharmacology*, 34 (10): 1079–1085. https://doi.org/10.1177/0269881120919957.

Rosenberg, M. B. 2003. *Nonviolent Communication: A Language of Life*. PuddleDancer Press.

Ross, Stephen, Anthony Bossis, Jeffrey Guss, Gabrielle Agin-Liebes, Tara Malone, Barry Cohen, Sarah E. Mennenga et al. 2016. "Rapid and Sustained Symptom Reduction Following Psilocybin Treatment for Anxiety and Depression in Patients with Life-Threatening Cancer: A Randomized Controlled Trial." *Journal of Psychopharmacology*, 30 (12): 1165–1180. https://doi.org/10.1177/0269881116675512.

Rotter, J. B. 1966. "Generalized Expectancies for Internal Versus External Control of Reinforcement." *Psychological Monographs: General and Applied*, 80 (1): 1–28.

Rushkoff, Douglas. 2022. *Survival of the Richest*. London: Scribe Publications.

Schwartz, Richard. 1995. *Internal Family Systems Therapy*. New York: Guilford Press.

Schwartz, Richard. 2013. *Parts Work: An Illustrated Guide to Your Inner Life*. CreateSpace Independent Publishing Platform.

Schwartz, Richard. 2020. *No Bad Parts: Healing Trauma and Restoring Wholeness with the Internal Family Systems Model*. Louisville: Sounds True Inc.

Shanon, Benny. 2002. *The Antipodes of the Mind: Charting the Phenomenology of the Ayahuasca Experience*. Oxford University Press.

Shiroma, Paulo R., Brian Johns, Michael Kuskowski, Joseph Wels, Paul Thuras, C. Sophia Albott, and Kelvin O. Lim. 2014. "Augmentation of response and remission to serial intravenous subanesthetic ketamine in treatment resistant depression." *Journal of Affective Disorders*, 155: 123–129.

Shulgin, Ann and Alexander Shulgin. 1995. *PiHKAL: A Chemical Love Story*. Berkeley, California: Transform Press.

Shulgin, Ann and Alexander Shulgin. 1997. *TiHKAL: The Continuation*. Berkeley, California: Transform Press.

Singh JB, Fedgchin M, Daly EJ, De Boer P, Cooper K, Lim P, Pinter C, Murrough JW, Sanacora G, Shelton RC, Kurian B, Winokur A, Fava M, Manji H, Drevets WC, Van Nueten L. A Double-Blind, Randomized, Placebo-Controlled, Dose-Frequency Study of Intravenous Ketamine in Patients With Treatment-Resistant Depression. Am J Psychiatry. 2016 Aug 1;173(8):816-26. doi: 10.1176/appi.ajp.2016.16010037. Epub 2016 Apr 8. PMID: 27056608.

Stensaas, Martin and Sunny Strasburg. *The Invention of Discovery*, Acrylic on oil on canvas. Accessed March 21, 2023. https://www.martinstensaas.com/collaborativepaintings#/invention-of-discovery/

Strassman, R. J. 2001. *DMT: The Spirit Molecule: A Doctor's Revolutionary Research into the Biology of Near-Death and Mystical Experiences*. South Paris, Maine: Park Street Press.

Tedeschi, R.G. and L. G. Calhoun. 1996. "The Posttraumatic Growth Inventory: Measuring the Positive Legacy of Trauma." *Journal of Traumatic Stress*, 9 (3): 455–71. https://doi.org/10.1007/BF02103658.

Turner, D. M., C. E. Coggins, and P. F. Daley. 2015. "Salvia Divinorum: An Ethnopharmacologic Review." *Journal of Psychoactive Drugs*, 47 (1): 16–27.

Van Edwards, Vanessa. 2017. *Captivate: The Science of Succeeding with People*. Alberta: Portfolio Publishing.

Van Etten, M. L. and S. Taylor. 1998. "Comparative Efficacy of Treatments for Post-Traumatic Stress Disorder: A Meta-Analysis." *Database of Abstracts of Reviews of Effects (DARE)*. Accessed March 21, 2023. https://www.ncbi.nlm.nih.gov/books/NBK67406/

Von Franz, Marie-Louise. 1974. *The feminine in fairy tales*. Spring Publications.

Von Franz, Marie-Louise. 2001. *Creation Myths*, Rev. ed. Boston: Shambhala.

Warneken, Felix and Michael Tomasello. 2006. "Altruistic Helping in Human Infants and Young Chimpanzees." *Science*, 311 (5765): 1301–3. https://doi.org/10.1126/science.1121448.

Wasson, R. Gordon. 1957. "Seeking the Magic Mushroom." *LIFE* (May 13, 1957): 100–120.

Waters, E. and E. M. Cummings. 2000. "A Secure Base from Which to Explore Close Relationships." *Child Development*, 71 (1): 164–72. https://doi.org/10.1111/1467-8624.00130.

Way, Maclain and Chapman Way, directors. *Wild Wild Country*. Duplass Brothers Productions, 2018. 1 hr., 4 min.

WHO. (2021). WHO model list of essential medicines - 22nd list. Geneva: World Health Organization.

Wilkinson, S. T., E. D. Ballard, M. H. Bloch, S. J. Mathew, J. W. Murrough, A. Feder, P. Sos, G. Wang, and G. 2018. "The effect of a single dose of intravenous ketamine on suicidal ideation: a systematic review and individual participant data meta-analysis." *The American Journal of Psychiatry*, 175 (2): 150. https://doi.org/10.1176/appi.ajp.2017.17040472.

Wolf, Ernest. S. 1988. *Treating the Self: Elements of Clinical Self Psychology*. New York: Guilford Press.

Yehuda, Rachel. 2002. "Post-Traumatic Stress Disorder." *The New England Journal of Medicine*, 346: 108–114. https://doi.org/10.1056/NEJMra012941.

Young-Eisendrath, Polly and Terence Dawson (eds.). 2008. *The Cambridge Companion to Jung*. Cambridge University Press.

RESOURCES

Further Reading Online

— "The Guru Syndrome." *Psychology Today.* www.psychologytoday.com/us/blog/out-the-darkness/201904/the-guru-syndrome

— "EMDR Float Back Method." *EMDR Therapy Volusia.* emdrtherapyvolusia.com/wp-content/uploads/2016/12/Floatback_and_Float.pdf

— "Float Back." *Compassion Works.* compassionworks.com/wp-content/uploads/2018/10/Floatback9.pdf

— "What are NMDA Receptors?" *News-Medical.net.* www.news-medical.net/life-sciences/What-are-NMDA-Receptors.aspx

— "Psilocybin Rewires Brain in People with Depression." *UC San Francisco.* www.ucsf.edu/news/2022/04/422606/psilocybin-rewires-brain-people-depression

— "Positive Transference." *Positive Psychology.* positivepsychology.com/countertrans

— General Resources

— Sunny Strasburg, LMFT Therapy website: sunnystrasburgtherapy.com

— Sunny Strasburg, LMFT Retreats: www.sunnystrasburgretreats.com

— Multidisciplinary Association for Psychedelic Studies: maps.org

— Johns Hopkins Center for Psychedelic and Consciousness Research: hopkinspsychedelic.org

— EMDRIA EMDR information and training: www.emdria.org

— IFS Institute: Internal Family Systems information and training: ifs-institute.com

— Erowid: www.erowid.org

— Paul Stamets: paulstamets.com

— The Beckley foundation: www.beckleyfoundation.org

- *How to Change Your Mind*, Michael Pollan: michaelpollan.com/books/how-to-change-your-mind
- Heffter Research: www.heffter.org
- ICEERS: www.iceers.org
- The Ancestor Project: www.theancestorproject.com
- United States Drug Enforcement Administration (DEA): www.dea.gov/drug-information/drug-scheduling
- Free online Myers-Briggs personality test: www.16personalities.com/free-personality-test

Trauma and EMDR Information

- *The Body Keeps the Score: Brain, Mind, and Body in the Healing of Trauma* by Dr. Bessel van der Kolk M.D.
- MarcoPagani study: sunnystrasburgtherapy.com/wp-content/uploads/2019/04/MarcoPagani.pdf
- Inside EMDR article: sunnystrasburgtherapy.com/wp-content/uploads/2019/04/Inside-EMDR-Article.pdf
- EMDRIA: www.emdria.org
- EMDR Frequently Asked Questions: www.emdr.com/frequent-questions
- How AIP (Adaptive Information Processing) works: www.drsoniamaxwell.com/indiv/emdr/emdr032AIP-drm.html
- *Waking the Tiger: Healing Trauma* by Dr. Peter Levine.
- ACE Study on how trauma affects adults: www.cdc.gov/violenceprevention/acestudy/about.html
- Peter Levine how trauma works in the brain: youtu.be/nmJDkzDMllc
- *The Wisdom of Trauma* by Gabor Maté

Attachment Styles

– https://youtu.be/e9EgUvfgojY
– https://youtu.be/OYoIVCHVwKI

Audio Books on Attachment

– *How to Heal Your Attachment Wounds* by Diane Poole Heller
– *Attached* by Amir Levine and Rachel Heller

Gottman Institute Information

– The Gottman Institute: www.gottman.com
– Gottman Repair that Works Video: www.youtube.com/watch?v=SqPvgDYmJnY
– Gottman Card Decks App: www.gottman.com/iphone-apps-2

Podcasts

– Psychedelics Today: https://psychedelicstoday.com/2023/03/30/pt402-sunny-strasburg/
– Dangerous Wisdom: https://podcasts.apple.com/us/podcast/k-wholeness-dialogue-with-sunny-strasburg-on/id1617741528?i=1000593897703
– Leadership Launchpad Project: https://podcasts.apple.com/ca/podcast/the-heros-journey-with-sunny-strasburg/id1530978841?i=1000604904270
– See You on The Other Side: https://www.audible.com/pd/20-Psychedelic-Trauma-Therapy-with-Sunny-Strasburg-LMFT-Podcast/B0BDX9KZDL?ref=a_pd_See-Yo_cI_lAsin_2_6
– Relationships Alive: https://youtu.be/y4EJuXyH8To

Books on Relationships

- *What Makes Love Last?* by Dr. John Gottam
- *Raising an Emotionally Intelligent Child* by Dr. John Gottam

Women's Resources

- *Women Who Run with Wolves* by Clarissa Pinkola Estés
- *Untie the Strong Woman: Blessed Mother's Immaculate Love for the Wild Soul* by Clarissa Pinkola Estés
- *Mother Night Myths, Stories and Teachings for Learning to See in the Dark* by Clarissa Pinkola Estés
- *Untamed* by Glennon Doyle

Internal Family Systems

- *Internal Family Systems* by Richard Schwartz
- *No Bad Parts* by Richard Schwartz

Psychedelic-Assisted Therapy Books and Research

- Psilocybin reduces anxiety and depression in cancer patients: https://www.ncbi.nlm.nih.gov/pmc/articles/PMC5367557/
- Ketamine to treat depression, PTSD and anxiety: https://www.scientificamerican.com/custom-media/mount-sinai/in-an-old-drug-new-hope-for-depression
- MDMA reduces social anxiety in autistic adults: https://maps.org/research/mdma/anxiety/autism
- Michael Pollen interview: https://singularityhub.com/2019/03/31/the-new-science-of-psychedelics-a-tool-for-changing-our-minds

- *The Psychedelic Experience* by Timothy Leary
- *LSD and the Mind of the Universe* by Christopher Bache
- *The Transpersonal Vision* by Stanislov Grof
- *Sacred Knowledge* by Bill Richards
- *The Psychedelic Explorer's Guide* by James Fadiman
- *How to Change Your Mind* by Michael Pollan

Apps and Online Resources to Supplement or When You Cannot Afford Therapy

- https://greatist.com/grow/resources-when-you-can-not-afford-therapy
- https://www.psychologytoday.com/us/blog/the-angry-therapist/201802/7-tips-dealing-life-if-you-cant-afford-therapist
- Apps for mental health rated: https://onemindpsyberguide.org/apps/

Philosophy and Psychology Books

- *Memories, Dreams and Reflections* by Carl G. Jung
- *The Power of Myth* by Joseph Campbell
- *Team Human* by Douglas Rushkoff
- *Survival of the Richest* by Douglas Rushkoff
- *Sapiens* by Yuval Harari
- *Homo Deus* by Yuval Harari
- *Captivate* by Vanessa van Edwards
- *The Future Human* by Jean Houston
- *Erasing Death* by Sam Parnia
- *The Ministry of the Future* by Kim Stanley Robinson
- *Real Magic* by Dean Radon
- *Dying to Be Me* by Anita Moorjani

- *Brave New World* by Aldous Huxley
- *The Varieties of Religious Experience* by William James
- *Codependent No More* by Melody Beattie

USA Ketamine Clinic Directories

- ketamineclinicsdirectory.com
- www.askp.org/directory/

IMPRINT

The Theradelic Approach
Psychedelic Therapy: Perspective, Preparation, and Practice

© Sunny Strasburg, LMFT 2023

ISBN: 979-8-218-22007-5
Published by Sunny Strasburg, LMFT 2023

Editors: Deborah Emmitt, Jane Gerhard, and Dr Jeffrey Becker, M.D.
Project management: Sunny Strasburg, LMFT
Cover: Sunny Strasburg, LMFT and Janine Milstrey
Layout: Janine Milstrey
Proofreading: Elizabeth Horstman

For more information, please visit:
www.sunnystrasburgtherapy.com and www.thetheradelicapproach.com